WALLPAPER

WALLPAPER

Brenda Greysmith

STUDIO VISTA
LONDON

A Studio Vista book published by
Cassell & Collier Macmillan Publishers Ltd,
35 Red Lion Square, London WC1R 4SG
and at Sydney, Auckland, Toronto, Johannesburg,
an affiliate of
Macmillan Publishing Co., Inc.,
New York.

ISBN   0 289 70718 8

Designed by Anthony Cohen
Set in 11pt Garamond
Printed by Colour Reproductions Ltd., Billericay, Essex.
Bound by R. J. Acfords Ltd., Chichester, Sussex.

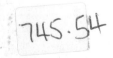

Contents

Acknowledgements

ERY many people have been involved to a greater or lesser degree in my researches for this book. In some cases the people I here take pleasure in thanking encouraged or merely helped to eliminate one of the many lines of enquiry which I found it necessary to pursue. In other cases they provided information, samples or photographs, and often volunteered themselves for a formidable amount of work.

In particular I would like to mention Christopher Allan of the Whitworth Art Gallery, Manchester, who patiently unrolled hundreds of samples with great good humour and arranged for many photographs to be taken. I am also extremely grateful to Jean Hamilton of the Victoria and Albert Museum, London, who shared her knowledge and time unstintingly, and very kindly read over the manuscript. In addition, I would like to single out Michael Mosesson and John Waterer of the Museum of Leathercraft, now at Walsall, for the interest they showed and the information they supplied.

My thanks go to the numerous embassies and wallpaper firms who responded kindly to my enquiries, and to all the following people for their various contributions:

Katarina Agren of the Västerbottens Museum, Umea, Sweden; John Bradshaw of the Ferens Art Gallery, Hull; the Staff of the Royal Pavilion, Brighton; the Staff of the Print Room and Library of the British Museum, London; Sally Chappell of the Victoria and Albert Museum, London, Photographic Studio; the Staff of the Clive House Museum, Shrewsbury; Michael Darby and the Staff of the Print Room and Library of the Victoria and Albert Museum; Germaine Desguin of the Groupement des Fabricants de Papier Peints de Belgique; Samuel J. Dornsife; Mrs Murray Douglas of Brunschwig and Fils, New York; Audrey Emerson of the Irish Georgian Society; Sterling Emerson of the Shellburne Museum, Vermont; Shelagh Ford of the American Museum in Britain, Bath; the Staff of the Bibliothèque Forney, Paris; Mrs Catherine Lynn Frangiamore and the Staff of the Cooper Hewitt Museum of Design, New York; Christopher Gilbert and Michael Sheppard of Temple Newsam House, Leeds; Norah Gillow of the William Morris Gallery, Walthamstow; Charles R. Gracie and Sons, New York; the Hagley Museum, Delaware; Hans et Fils, Paris;

the Library Staff of Hornsey College of Art; Jacqueline Jacque, Musée de l'Impression sur Étoffes, Mulhouse; Odile Kammerer of the Musée des Arts Décoratifs, Paris; the Museum für Kunst und Gewerbe, Hamburg; Maxine Leonard of the Geffrye Museum; the Staff of the London Library; Marburger Tapetenfabrik, Kassel; Markisches Museum, Berlin; Dr Ernst Wolfgang Mick of the Deutsches Tapetenmuseum, Kassel; Barbara Morris of the Victoria and Albert Museum; Jiří Mucha and his secretary, Marta Kadlečíková; the Staff of the Bibliothèque National, Paris; New York Public Library; Richard Nylander of the Society for the Preservation of New England Antiquities; Osborne and Little of London; Bruno Passamani of the Museo Biblioteca e Archive di Bassano del Grappa; Stanley Pilkington of Potters, Darwen; Eddie Pond of the Wallpaper Manufacturers Limited, London; the Staff of the National Portrait Gallery, London; Salubra A.G., Basel, Switzerland; the Staff of Shrewsbury Reference Library; Irene Sigurdsson of the Stockholm Stadsmuseum; the State Russian Museum, Moscow; Poul Strømstad of the National Museets, Denmark; Annika Tyrfelt of the Nordiska Museet, Stockholm; Roger Underhill; Heidi Weber, the Corbusier Centre, Zurich; and the Staff of the Whitworth Art Gallery, Manchester.

I should also like to thank Helen McDonald for her very reliable assistance during the period of my researching and writing this book, and my husband for his encouragement.

Introduction

WALLPAPERS deserve a searching look, over as wide a geographical area and as long a timescale as possible. The history of wallpaper stretches back further than most people imagine, and it is a subject, moreover, that is less researched than most other aspects of decorative art. Many of the museums that I contacted, although they do hold wallpaper collections, have no photographic records, nor indeed any form of cataloguing or other explanatory literature. Many collections are dominated by modern reproductions of William Morris designs. French and English wallpapers seem to be well represented in every country, but indigenous work is often more difficult to find. The only museum completely devoted to wallpaper is the Deutsches Tapetenmuseum in Kassel, set up primarily by German wallpaper dealers and manufacturers in 1923. Inevitably then my survey will be to some extent unbalanced and incomplete; as research continues and more material becomes available, the missing pieces of the puzzle will be added. But it should be pointed out in fairness to the museums that wallpapers are among the most difficult of artefacts to store and display. No museum has the money or facilities to display all its collection, even if it wished to. And the fragile rolls and fragments, assorted in size and quality, some still attached to their plaster, cause much worry to the staff who are obliged to unpack or unroll them whenever any research is to be carried out.

Despite language difficulties, some of the foreign museums I approached responded extremely helpfully. Yet the map still contains some very large blank areas, one of the largest of which is Russia. Turgenev's *First Love,* published in 1860, provides in one passage a tantalizing account of wallpaper manufacture:

> In the lodge was a tiny wallpaper factory . . . Village boys with pinched faces jumped on wooden levers and forced them on to the square blocks of the presses, and in this way by the weight of their shrunken bodies stamped the brightly coloured patterns on the paper.

Wallpaper also appears as a background in several Russian paintings of domestic interiors. Yet it proved impossible to follow up these clues. Disappointingly, this was also true of China, which plays a significant part in the history of western wallpaper but seems unwilling to cast any further light on its evolving styles or on the attitudes of its manufacturers.

The scope of this book, then, is partly dictated by the limited information it is possible for the researcher to gather. Similar restrictions of supply have meant that the illustrations, although representative of every period, are more numerous for the later developments of wallpaper, since naturally there were far more extant examples here from which to make a choice, and the material was in better condition. But there is yet a further boundary to the range of a survey like this, and that is drawn at the discretion of the individual researcher, rather than by the requirements of availability. The problem is to decide which of the many closely related types of interior decoration can be mentioned within the confines of the term 'wallpaper'. For the floor-to-ceiling, corner-to-corner, totally continuous use of wallpaper that is so common today is only one of a multitude of styles. Small cut-out motifs, for instance, have been popular quite recently, and so have panels, borders and friezes. Among the more extreme variations are small hand-printed or painted sheets of paper, possibly manufactured for some other purpose and sometimes verging on fine-art prints or paintings. Ceiling papers, commercial posters and temporary, free-hanging paper decorations belong to the same capacious species. My own inclination has been to give due weight to these variants. Their history can scarcely be separated from that of the mainstream developments in the use and design of wallpaper, and what is more, they are useful in indicating ways in which wallpaper today might be used more imaginatively and flexibly.

Despite—or perhaps because of—the fascination that wallpaper can exert it is one of the most potentially irritating of the decorative arts. People react to it very emotionally. Oscar Wilde commented on his deathbed: 'My wallpaper is killing me—one of us must go.' Much the same sentiment was voiced by Vallance in the *Magazine of Art* in 1904:

> It may be asserted without exaggeration that in hundreds and hundreds of cases the sufferings of the sick are aggravated by the surroundings which they themselves have unwittingly chosen for the altogether opposite purpose of decoration.

In addition to this, wallpaper has had to cope at various times in its history with long periods of unpopularity, a burden that has never befallen, say, printed textiles. Many people prefer paint or self-coloured paper to a pattern for their walls, although from a purely practical point of view a pattern or broken colour looks cleaner for longer. Another school of thought is that which believes that the best wallpaper is subordinate to the contents of a room, merely an unobtrusive background to the furniture and living occupants. More damaging still to the prestige of wallpaper is the sort of wry disparagement implicit in George Moore's attack on Henry Cole's art schools: they were 'primarily intended,' Moore wrote, 'as schools of design where the sons and daughters of the people would be taught how to design wallpapers.'* Substitute any other form of applied art

* Quoted from Fiona McCarthy *All Things Bright and Beautiful: Design in Britain 1830 to Today* Allen and Unwin, London 1972

9

here and the bite of the remark would be lost. Wallpaper has been the subject of derision in a unique way.

This is unjust. It is true that there is a need for patterns that do not harass the eye, for even a seemingly inoffensive unit can become intolerable when multiplied. Yet, properly planned and designed, wallpaper can have a powerful cosmetic effect on a room. Its keenest supporters would say that it was in itself a skin without which our walls would reveal the crude materials of their construction. William Morris, who always covered his own rooms with wallpaper, decreed in his lecture on 'The Lesser Arts of Life':

> Whatever you have in your rooms think of the walls, for they are that which makes your house your home, and if you do not make some sacrifice in their favour you will find your chambers have a kind of makeshift lodging-house look about them, however rich and handsome your moveables may be.

Wallpaper can not only give a fine finish to a room, it can also dictate a mood more effectively than any other element in furnishing. It can be rich and luxurious, pretty and peaceful, gay, mysterious, exciting, even educational. Walls patterned with leafy groves, through which in the imagination one is invited to wander, or with tableaux from history, which the mind's eye can animate, are less common than they were. But that does not mean that wallpaper today has not a potentially exciting future in other, perhaps unpredictable directions.

In its pioneer days, wallpaper was under the control of the artisan, the craftsman printer, whose understanding and feeling for the simple processes used resulted in genuine and sympathetic designs. As the popularity of the product increased, the change in the size and sophistication of the market led to the dilution of the folk art feeling in wallpaper and the introduction of elaborate decorative schemes worked out by designers of complete interiors. One of the most notable of these was Chippendale. With the Industrial Revolution, the manufacturers became the main arbiters of taste in wallpaper, since the principal desiderata at this time were technical prowess and the ability to produce large quantities. There followed from the professional art critics the inevitable reaction to this trend, and the result was a renewed blossoming in wallpaper design. The emphasis was taken away from the industrialist and placed upon the artist designer who, unlike the early artisan, was concerned with design more as an abstract conception than as an acquired skill directly emerging from a close technical knowledge of printing techniques. Thus, different periods in the history of wallpaper have been influenced by different elements in society, and this is mirrored in the organization of this book. Each chapter has a particular flavour, depending on the particular blend of individual workmanship and large-scale manufacture that it reflects.

The situation now seems balanced between industry and the individual designers. The manufacturers became rather impersonal during the first half of the century; their sheer size and the amounts of both wallpaper and money involved led to an attitude of cautious conservatism which discouraged any radical changes in the types of design they produced. But now, once again, small firms are setting up in which designers can oversee their work in production, and greater gambles can be taken without fear of enormous repercussions. It is my hope that this look at the many varied stages in the history of wallpaper may help to open up avenues for exploration and stimulate a new interest in its future development.

Beginnings

TO search for the beginning of anything as ephemeral as wallpaper is rather like looking for a needle in a haystack. The chances of finding early examples extant are extremely remote, and the quest is complicated by a knotty problem of nomenclature: wallpaper is a term of relatively recent origin, and many of the items discussed in this book could also be considered as paintings or prints, and there is much too that has been pirated from other uses, for example lining papers for chests and boxes, or book endpapers. For every piece of wallpaper that remains, hundreds more have been lost. Of all the decorative arts, wallpaper is probably the most vulnerable to damp and destruction. It suffers not only from frequent attacks of redecoration and the eventual decay or demolition of the houses where it was hung, but also from more momentous disasters like the Great Fire of London of 1666 (which few early wallpapers survived) and the Second World War.

From the very beginning, wallpaper has been regarded mostly, though not always, as a poor substitute for more luxurious and expensive mural decorations, and therefore has not been preserved with any great care. It has never been thought worthy of being handed down as an heirloom. The low regard in which wallpaper has been held is reflected to some extent in its frequent imitation of other materials.

Soon after man surrounded himself with walls, he started to think about ways of decorating them, and over the centuries that elapsed before the evolution of wallpaper, the decorations he used became more elaborate, more luxurious and more skilfully made. When wallpaper at last became a practicable mural decoration it was greatly influenced in both design and technology by existing modes of wallcovering. It acquired an imitative, eclectic character from which it has never quite freed itself. Starting with animal skins, cave paintings and woven grasses, wall decoration evolved through periods of elaborate stonework, richly embroidered draperies of wool and linen, carved and painted wood-panelling, and tapestries, silks and serges. These materials, and to an even greater degree printed textiles and embossed and gilded leather, are largely responsible for the way both ancient and contemporary wallpapers have looked.

Of course, many of the less durable of these antecedents, like the

1
Danish wallpaper, *c.* 1890, imitating
woven material.
Nationalmuseet, Copenhagen.

wallpapers they have influenced, have perished. Tapestries have survived
in greater numbers than other woven hangings; the silks, velvets and
damasks have mainly gone. Some embroidery was done in imitation of true
tapestry—the so-called Bayeux Tapestry is an example—but the laborious
nature of the work involved made large-scale projects of this kind
extremely rare. At a more humble level, the Anglo-Saxons sewed
homespun lengths of woollen cloth together to form hangings, which
helped to insulate their houses. These too were often embroidered, to
illustrate folk tales and myths.

England was producing tapestries early. In 1382 Richard II granted a
licence to Cosmo Gentilis, the Pope's Receiver of Revenues in England, to
export cloths of various kinds and colours duty free. One of the shipments
to be made under this arrangement was of six pieces of tapestry, of a green
ground powered with roses, a present from the King to the Pope. The art
was brought to perfection by the time of Henry VIII, and one of its most
prestigious designers at this time is said to have been Holbein. In the reign

13

2
German canvas wallhanging, *c.*1660, depicting a boar hunt. Printed with a single application of flock.
Whitworth Art Gallery,
University of Manchester.

of James I a large tapestry factory was established by Sir Francis Crane at Mortlake. It flourished for a while but came to grief eventually in the ravages of the Civil War.

Occasionally tapestries were commissioned with exactly specified dimensions to match the wall spaces to be covered. More often though they seem to have been bought in sets of three or five, and when hung they were carried round the corners of the room. Wealthy Europeans in the late seventeenth and eighteenth centuries patronized the tapestry makers of Brussels and those of the famous French manufactory the Gobelins (founded in 1662) as well as English craftsmen. In Brussels, spaces were often left in the middle of the top border of tapestries for the coats-of-arms or ciphers of their purchasers. Similar heraldic motifs were to be found in contemporary wallpapers.

Other fabrics used to cover the walls of the comfortably off had a comparable impact on designs for paper hangings. In Germany, linen hangings were especially popular, and there are several interesting extant examples of this vogue, some of which are flocked. Flocking, a technique still used in both wallpaper and textile production, was initially employed to imitate more costly materials, particularly velvet. Links between wallpaper and printed textiles still exist in much the same form today: designs are shared by both products, sometimes with the idea that they should be used together in a room with an integrated design, and sometimes merely so that the same blocks can be utilized as a matter of economic expediency. The influence of silks can be seen in the predilection of wallpaper manufacturers, right from the beginning, for reflective surfaces, either in the golds and silvers they often used or in the use of mica and other substances and techniques to give a translucent shine to the paper.

One of the more important debts of wallpaper to other forms of decoration is that owed to leather hangings (see Colour Plate 1). Many early wallpaper makers also worked in this medium, and some of the techniques, and again the motifs, were common to both trades. Leather hangings originate from the Libyan town of Ghadames and when they started being produced in Spain, especially in Cordoba, they were given the name of *guademeci* (also known as 'Cordovan leather'). In Eastern countries goatskin dressed with alum was used and was reputedly as soft as silk. In Europe the usual material was sheepskin. The *guademeci* were painted with gold or silver foil, though sometimes a yellow varnish was applied to tin foil to simulate gold. The surface was ornamented by small punches which caused the otherwise bland surface to glitter. Later, metal plates engraved with imitation stamping took the place of handwork, and low relief embossing became fashionable. It was probably not until the early seventeenth century that embossing was done with wooden moulds in a modified printing press. Stamped leather, however, was found in the tomb of Tutenkhamun, and although there are no surviving hangings before the

3
Wallpainting, c. 1580, from
Coldharbour Farm, Kent.
Roger Underhill.

fifteenth century, there seems no reason why simple ones should not have been produced as early as the eighth and ninth centuries.

Italy, especially Venice, had a thriving trade in *guademeci* during the Renaissance, and England and the Low Countries also produced work of considerable quality. Holland took up the industry late and continued to produce leather hangings into the eighteenth century, by which time they had become rather unfashionable elsewhere. A record was made in 1578 of rooms in Edinburgh Castle, occupied by Mary Queen of Scots, being ornamented with 'elevin tapestries of gilt leder'. Many examples show the use of a distinctive red dye, which is probably madder, since the Cordovans, extremely proud of their standards, passed an ordinance in 1543 prohibiting the use of any other dye. Infringement of this law, or of another one that forbade the use of inferior metal foils, carried severe penalties, sometimes even death.

Another art form present at the nebulous beginnings of wallpaper—a precursor, rival and influence—was wallpainting. Fresco seems too grand a word, for although the larger and more ambitious paintings did have an effect on wallpapers, especially in the nineteenth century when technical progress made possible the most amazing feats, it was the small and unpretentious secular work of the late medieval itinerant painters which made the greatest impact. In some countries, America and Scandinavia for example, this form of folk art continued for many years and wallpaper remained a luxury beyond the means of ordinary rural families. Stencils of heavy paper stiffened with oil and paint were often used to facilitate the work of these craftsmen. In exchange for bed and board and a small sum, they would rapidly decorate walls and sometimes floors with bold colours and designs very similar to those popular in wallpapers of the time.

Wallpaper motifs also drew upon a particular style of embroidery that lent itself to reproduction by block printing. This was 'blackwork', the name given to the method of embroidery in one colour—normally black, though sometimes red—which seems to have been known in England in the late fifteenth century. It can be seen on many clothes and decorated articles of the period. In later examples intricate diaper patterns and free scrolling stems enclose flower and leaf motifs. The fashion for this style was widespread in Elizabethan England, so much so that pattern books for ladies to work from were specially imported in large numbers at the beginning of the sixteenth century. Not many survive, since the pattern was pricked directly through the paper on to the material and this dramatically shortened the lives of the books. This vogue coincided with the beginning of printing, and it seems likely that spare sheets of designs from the pattern books, printed from engraved wooden blocks, were sold off by the printers for decorative purposes. The blocks were doubtless used also for both textile and paper wallhangings. Because the printing was in black only, colours would be painted on afterwards, sometimes with a stencil.

4
Blackwork embroidery on a pillow case.

Victoria and Albert Museum,
London.

By this time paper had a long history behind it, dating back to around 2500 B.C. (there is an Egyptian 'paper' scroll of this date now to be found in the Louvre, Paris). It was primitively made at first from the stems of papyrus reeds which grew thickly along the banks of the Nile, but later it began to be produced from other materials. The Chinese used bamboo at first and many other early paper-makers favoured bark; the Anglo-Saxons used the bark of birch trees. It is significant that many of the words now relating to books and libraries are based etymologically on the ancient words for bark and bamboo. But paper as we know it today is believed to have been first produced in China in the early second century and was made of bark and linen rags. From China, knowledge of paper-making passed to Japan around A.D. 600 and since then the Japanese have always been renowned for their high quality and specialized papers. The Chinese also passed on the technique to the Arabs, in about A.D. 750, and from them it was gradually diffused westwards.

Manufacture spread slowly. Paper mills were built at Baghdad and Damascus, and the Moors, who invaded Spain in 1150, built a mill in North Valencia. A little later the French, with Spanish assistance, built their first mill, and later they became the most prolific paper-makers of the Middle Ages. In 1276 paper began to be produced in Italy, and during the next two hundred years it spread to most other European countries. It reached Russia in the sixteenth century and America and Canada in the seventeenth. Before long, attempts were made to produce paper without rags, and several eighteenth-century text books dealing with the subject are still in existence—some of them containing samples of paper made from such materials as nettles, hops and moss.

Wallpaper, like paper itself, is usually believed to be a Chinese invention. John Hilditch remarks in Sugden and Edmonson's *History of Wallpaper* that Chinese walls were often lined with wood and handmade paper, sometimes crudely decorated and coated with lacquer, as early as A.D. 200. Paper designs were also produced very early for funeral rites, and copies of them were hung on walls. Although their significance was partly religious, they also had a strong decorative quality. In some houses the

5
Lining or wallpaper in the blackwork style, seventeenth century.
Ashmolean Museum, Oxford.

6
Chinese Album Leaf mounted as a
hanging scroll showing a Mynah bird.
Ink and colour on silk, fourteenth
century.
Victoria and Albert Museum,
London.

walls were papered and then covered with free-hand drawings: one
recorded example showed a genealogical tree reaching back two hundred
years. Scrolls of either silk or paper were also hung on walls in Chinese
houses, and probably derived from painted and inscribed banners serving a
festive purpose. They were entirely temporary and were frequently
changed for special occasions. Although woodcut techniques were known
in China seven hundred years before they were first discovered in Europe,
printing was rarely employed for these articles. The earliest designs
pictured deities and priests, but during the T'ang period (A.D. 618-906) the
repertoire was extended to include animals, flowers and landscapes.

The Japanese have used paper extensively in their houses too, but again
in a way which seems bizarre to western eyes. Until recently, rice paper

7
Swedish wallhanging, painted on woven material by Gustave Reuter 1699–1783, a soldier and painter from Halsingland. The figure is King Carl XII greatly loved by his soldiers, and the text reads, 'Carolus must be remembered he was the greatest man in the world and killed many enemies'.

Nordiska Museet, Stockholm.

was placed over windows to give a creamy light and stretched over the fusuma, the dividing screens between rooms. Sometimes the fusuma were covered with a dull gold or enlivened with a faint landscape or a decorative drawing of birds and flowers; sometimes the paper was tinted or painted with ideographs.

In Europe, as in China, painted paper decorations preceded printed ones. Phyllis Ackerman records that in 1481 Louis XI paid a painter and illuminator named Jean Bourdichon the sum of twenty-four livres for painting fifty rolls of paper in blue with the inscription 'Misericordias Domini in Aeternum Cantabo' and three angels. Painted and gilded paper decorations are known to have been brought out for the entry of Louis XII into Lyons. Other papers, often with biblical designs, are mentioned in various inventories, though they had to compete with painted cloths, which could be produced in greater lengths. Many of these early European hangings were purely temporary. Some had an ill-defined religious importance, although, as we see from one of the Swedish examples illustrated, the popularity of sacred subject matter began before long to decline in favour of the profane.

In Sweden painted wallhangings such as these continued to be produced well into the nineteenth century. They fell into two categories. Those produced in Northern Sweden, where wood was plentiful and houses large, were often displayed in rooms set aside specially for festive occasions. The hangings were adjusted to suit wall panels for which they were intended. The hangings made in Southern Sweden, on the other hand, were designed to fit above benches in the long, low kitchens, and as they were only brought out for religious festivals, the motifs retain more of their sacral character than elsewhere. Although they seem to be a distinctively Swedish phenomenon, these hangings do reflect something of the scale and figurative and symbolic quality of early wallpaper designs in England and France. They are also an interesting precursor of the wallpaper frieze.

8
Swedish wallhanging painted on woven material by Johannes Nilsson, Gyltige, Breared, Halland, south Swedish painter 1757–1827. It depicts Adam and Eve, the Wedding at Canaan, and Jesus coming into Jerusalem.
Nordiska Museet, Stockholm.

9
'Turkish Paper'—marbled paper
produced in south Germany, *c.* 1750.
Deutsches Tapetenmuseum.

In other European countries, France and Italy in particular, it was not painted hangings which played such an important part in the history of wallpaper so much as the making of domino papers. Various sorts of printed or painted papers were usually made by one firm—sometimes even by one man—because the market for each product was small. Thus, playing-card makers and printers were also *dominotiers,* or makers of decorated end-papers for books. Indeed, in France in about 1540 these jobs were grouped together by statute. Professional jealousy was organized into law: the *dominotier* printers were forbidden to use lettering and were limited to small sheets of paper. Few of their products are extant but those that do survive are often exquisite, especially the ones made in Italy. Like the Swedes with the paper hangings and the Dutch with their embossed leathers, the Italians, discovering that they had a particular aptitude for this sort of work, continued to practise it long after the general vogue had waned. Many of the papers were 'marbled'. This technique was first imported from Persia, and Sir Francis Bacon supplies an early description of it in his *Natural History* of 1623:

> The Turks have a very pretty art of chambletting paper which is not in use with us. They take divers oiled colours and put them severally (in drops) upon water and stir the water lightly and then wet the paper (being of some thickness) with it and the paper will be waved or veined like chamblet or marble.

Apart from these marbled papers, which were undoubtedly used as wallpapers—a habit which survives today—there was also a fashion for 'scratted' papers. These employed a technique whereby colour was simply flicked on to the surface at random with brushes.

It was England, as far as present researches show, that took the final step towards wallpaper production as we now know it. Early examples in the sixteenth century are few and far between, and the ones that do exist are often fragmentary and stained. What is generally accepted to be the earliest surviving example of wallpaper, certainly the first discovered in situ, is known as the 'Cambridge Fragments', so-called because it was found in 1911 in Christ's College, Cambridge. The design was an attempt to imitate contemporary woven material. It was printed by Hugo Goes, who worked in Beverley and York during the early sixteenth century, and his rebus can be seen on either side of the central pomegranate motif. The work is block printed on black, as most early designs were, on paper already once used, and it is this which dates the wallpaper from around 1509, for the text printed on the reverse refers to the first year of the reign of Henry VIII. Whether the proclamations on the reverse side were printed by Goes or Caxton's assistant and successor Wynkin de Worde, and were surplus, or whether they were the property of some other imaginative person, will probably remain a mystery.

Jean Hamilton of the Victoria and Albert Museum, London, has suggested that the Cambridge fragment may be predated by the example illustrated in Plate 11, a fragment depicting a royal crown surmounted by a crowned lion. The arms displayed could be those of either Henry VII or Henry VIII, but in any case it was certainly produced during the first half of the sixteenth century. Whether wallpapers and lining papers were made as separate products is impossible to say, but if they were, this particular

11
Fragment of wallpaper with Royal Crown, first half of the sixteenth century.
Victoria and Albert Museum, London.

10
A photographic reconstruction of the 'Cambridge Fragments'. Block printed in black by Hugo Goes, active early in the sixteenth century. Discovered in the Master's Lodge, Christ's College, Cambridge, in 1911.
Whitworth Art Gallery, University of Manchester.

example was probably produced as a lining paper, since from the very small area that remains it seems unlikely to have repeated well. As with some of the more emphatically patriotic papers, the design appears to be complete on one sheet of paper, in accord with a tradition that continued

24

13
Lining paper, block-printed black on
grey, English, early eighteenth
century.
Victoria and Albert Museum,
London.

12 *Opposite*
Fragment of lining paper showing
Tudor Rose, English *c.* 1550.
Victoria and Albert Museum,
London.

14
Fragment of lining paper including the
arms of the Haberdashers Company,
first half of the seventeenth century.
Printed from wood blocks.
Victoria and Albert Museum,
London.

well into the eighteenth century. There is a paper in this style bearing a
portrait of Charles II and Catherine of Braganza, dated 1662; and a later
one, from the first decade of the early eighteenth century, was discovered
lining a fine veneered chest of drawers owned by Lord Leverhulme. It
depicts a woman fishing, and is reminiscent of a type of design favoured by
needleworkers of that period. The paper showing the arms of the
Haberdasher's Company, dating from the first half of the seventeenth
century, is another example of this type. The rather formal and heraldic
nature of some of these early papers may have resulted because they were
often used, if not especially designed, for the lining of deed boxes. The
printing and painting of wallpapers doubtless continued in a sporadic and
relatively amateurish way throughout the sixteenth century. It seems likely
that its use was limited mostly to small areas such as chimney breasts and to
the linings of chests and cupboards, but these, of course, are the places
where wallpaper stands a better chance of surviving, so the conclusion is by

26

no means inevitable. Those who could afford to decorate their homes as they liked preferred materials that were more precious, less perishable and better tested. Wallpaper remained merely a popular art catering for those of little means.

One of the earliest papers, clearly Tudor and printed from a wooden block, was found adhering to the original wattle and daub in an old house at Besford Court, Worcestershire. The same high quality armorial design—black on a buff ground—was also found in a chest at Bristol and a deed box now in the Public Record Office. It has been dated between 1550 and 1575 and in any case must be prior to the accession of James I as the Scots arms do not appear. There are several examples, with slight variations, scattered throughout England, and they are also a number in similar styles, one of which bears the device of Ann Boleyn.

Most of these early papers seem to have been English but there is one tragic anecdote about Herman Schinkel from Delft which makes it indisputable that wallpapers were also being produced in Europe. Schinkel

15
Wallpaper from Besford Court
c.1550–75, still adhering to its plaster.
Now reproduced in Cole's present
range of wallpaper.
Victoria and Albert Museum,
London.

was convicted of printing and publishing books inimical to the Catholic Faith, and the death sentence was carried out in 1568. During his interrogation he was accused of printing certain ballads. He maintained in his defence that they had been printed by his servant, and that on discovering them he had thrown them in a corner, intending to print roses and stripes on the other side, to paper attics with. Sugden and Edmonson attribute certain work in England to Schinkel too, although the Victoria and Albert Museum dates it slightly later. In its characteristics of robustness and complexity of design, it bears a strong resemblance to many examples of Dutch embossed leather. Holland also produced a considerable number of plain papers coated with gold or silver leaf or metallic paint, and at the same time printed paper hangings were being manufactured in France, especially in Normandy, which was a thriving centre for the production of paper and linen.

Early English designs are invariably formal, being either heraldic in nature or with conventionalized motifs, in black usually but occasionally in red on white. Even the more flowing floral patterns were strongly indebted to embroidery and in no way aspired to be naturalistic.

By the end of the sixteenth century good quality polychrome work was making inroads upon the widespread popularity of one-colour letterpress printed wallpapers. One of two examples found in 1896 at Borden Hall, Sittingbourne, in Kent, dating from about 1600, was printed in black on a red ground, with jade green and turquoise foliage and flowers, and showed a noticeable Indian influence. It had been nailed to the plaster on the walls with large flatheaded nails. At the time of the discovery it was described and illustrated by Lindsay Butterfield, but later the fragments themselves disappeared, sadly reducing still further the already impoverished stock of extant experimental wallpapers from this crucial formative period.

16 *Opposite left*
Panel of wallhanging, flock on canvas, with black, green and orange apparently stencilled on a cream ground. Attributed by Sugden and Edmonson to Herman Schinkel of Delft (d.1568), but catalogued by the Victoria and Albert Museum as English seventeenth century.
Victoria and Albert Museum, London.

17 *Opposite right*
Lining paper with a design of small flowers over-printed from wood blocks on the proof sheets of an edition of Ovid's *Metamorphoses,* a relatively common practice for waste paper, English, *c.*1750.
Victoria and Albert Museum, London.

Blocks, Flocks and Butterflies

DURING the seventeenth century, painted and printed paper became increasingly popular as a decoration on walls, and more and more expertise came to be demanded in the manufacturing process. At the beginning of the century there were really no continuous 'repeats': each sheet was produced individually and formed a separate panel of the design, which seldom connected especially well with adjacent panels when they were placed side by side on the wall. Some papers, marbled ones for instance, were produced entirely by hand, but generally a

18
Reconstruction by Wyndham Payne from fragments of lining paper found in a box dated 1635. The motto *Ich Dien* and initials *H.P.* are those of Henry Frederick, created Prince of Wales in 1610.

Victoria and Albert Museum, London.

black outline was printed with an engraved wooden block and colours were added afterwards. The original design, drawn on a large sheet of paper the size of the final panel, was cut up into smaller squares in sizes convenient for the block makers. The blocks themselves, usually of pearwood, were fitted back together when carved and then laid face up, so that the separate parts of the design were once more contiguous. The blocks were then inked, covered with paper and rolled with a heavy hand roller. Sometimes colours were added, either freehand or by means of specially cut stencils, one for each colour.

Engraved metal plates were also used for wallpaper printing during this period. It is likely that this technique was for many years closely allied to the skills of wood block cutting: the trade cards of block printers—surely

19
Fleur de Lys wallpaper, French, seventeenth century. Block printed and handpainted in black, yellow and orange on a pale mauve ground. From the Castle of Marcoux, near Digne.
Musée des Arts Décoratifs, Paris.

not a task they would farm out—were often produced from engraved
plates and Matthias Darly, for instance, who worked in the eighteenth
century as a wallpaper manufacturer, was also known as the engraver of
some of the plates for Chippendale's *Director* (see page 48). 'Diana and
Actaeon' is an example of a wallpaper made in this way, and it is interesting
too as an early example of figurative paper. Actaeon is depicted at the very
moment of being turned into a stag, and the dogs nearby are just about to
devour him. The cruel metamorphosis is Actaeon's punishment for having
spied on the virgin goddess Diana while she was bathing.

Wood blocks, or methods involving stencils, were at this time being
used not only for straightforward printed wallpapers but also for 'flocked'
work. Woven fabrics had for some time been enriched in quality by the

33

22
Piece of flock wallpaper from the
lumber room between the hall and
chapel at All Soul's College, Oxford
in two shades of green, *c.* 1740.
Victoria and Albert Museum,
London.

addition of finely chopped silk or wool, and during the eighteenth century
flocked paper, similarly treated, enjoyed a tremendous vogue. This
relatively simple process created much interest, which has survived until
the present day. It is described at some length in Robert Dossie's book
Handmaid to the Arts, published in 1758, and the technique was
demonstrated in lectures given in London in the last century. Glue or
varnish was applied to the paper in the required pattern and then sprinkled
with powdered bits of material, and when the glue had dried, the excess
pieces were brushed off.

In 1620 Le Francois of Rouen was making flock papers as hangings in
imitation of silk weaves. Rouen was at this time the hub of the silk
industry, so there was ample waste readily available for use in the making
of flock wallpaper as soon as paper of adequate strength was being
produced. In England, Jerome Lanyer was granted a charter by Charles I
to manufacture flock papers, and he called his product 'Londriniana'.

21 *Opposite*
Late seventeenth century engraved
wallpaper depicting Diana and
Actaeon.
Victoria and Albert Museum,
London.

35

Lanyer may have been a Huguenot refugee, for his surname looks like an English version of Lanier, the French word for 'flocker'; but there is also a theory that he was a member of the famous Rouen family of court musicians of that name. Elsewhere, other materials were used to give the effect of gold and silver brocades. Johann Hauntsch of Nuremburg (1595-1670) (his descendants were still manufacturing at the beginning of the nineteenth century) was working with a variety of metal powders, each giving a slightly different colour, which he brushed on to the tacky varnish, probably with a hare's foot. Powder colours were used in this way to give a rough deep texture. But it was the ordinary wool flocks which became most popular, and it was in these that the English came to excel, to such a degree that the papers, sometimes known as 'tontisses', also became known as 'English papers', and other European countries pursued English supremacy avidly. The flock wall hanging attributed to Herman Schinkel (Plate 16) may confirm the theory that flocking was used for this purpose even earlier in Holland. This particular example is on canvas. In Germany, weightier hangings, particularly of linen, found great favour. The German Tapetenmuseum in Kassel, moreover, has many fine examples of embossed leather hangings, and experiments were being made in Germany at this time to produce paper impressed with a pattern in relief by techniques of leather embossing.

Flock papers designed over the next hundred years were produced with skill and preserved with care, so, despite the continuing predominance of cottons and linens, many have survived. The process itself may have strengthened them. Their strong link with woven materials ensured that the design repeated well vertically—though not necessarily laterally, for this was something which so far only a few designs had fortuitously achieved. Flock papers were eminently suitable then for wall coverings, and soon they became much displayed in English country houses. Cheaper than brocatelle, which they often imitated, but pleasing to the eye with their bold and stately designs, they continue to be popular even today. Many modern versions are rather alike in design and rather sombre in colouring, and this is perhaps due partly to a tendency to copy from remaining original examples, which are less likely to be pre-nineteenth century than Victorian, with a typically Victorian partiality for sober colours and complex designs. It comes as something of a shock to discover the bright and varied hues of the earlier, much livelier flocks. The colours used in these early days came from dyes that were well tried and researched, with an enormous variety of shades and a greater fastness to both light and damp than the printing inks and watercolours used in normal wallpaper production. In the example discovered at Welwick House, South Lynn, Norfolk, an iron mordant has apparently been used for the black flock, producing traces of rust on the paper.

Several examples survive from the beginning of the eighteenth century which remain unsurpassed. 1732 is the approximate date for the excellent flocks found at Clandon Park, Guildford, which have been carefully copied and restored (see Colour Plate 2). The alternating leather and flock paper found at Ivy House, Worcester, is undoubtedly earlier. This combination with leather seems to have been unusual, if not unique. As it was applied directly to the unplastered brickwork, it seems likely that it was part of the original decoration of the house, which was built in 1679 on the site of an old charnel-house near the cathedral. The leather, as so often, has a white ground and shows cherubs, once bronze in colour, that have been overlaid with silver foil and varnish. The flock wallpaper is crimson on a white ground and has the same design as an example found at Saltfleet Manor in Lincolnshire: a slightly fantastical architectural motif somewhat similar to that on the flock wallpaper from Hurlcote Manor, Towcester, which dates from the early eighteenth century.

A pleasing example of the increasing sophistication, fluidity and continuity of design that was evolving in other types of printed wallpapers also, is to be found in 'Birds and Poppies' (Colour Plate 3), a paper produced about 1700 by De Fourcroy, working at the rue Jacob-Saint Germain in Paris. It is interesting to compare it with the two English examples illustrated in Plate 27 and Colour Plate 4, for it bears a considerable likeness in colour to the one and in design to the other. Although the Jacobean design of the work has been dated as late as 1730, Sugden suggests on stylistic grounds that it could be a print from a much earlier block. The evidence seems to point to a cross-fertilizing effect upon

24
Flock wallpaper discovered at Welwick House, South Lynn, Norfolk. Pevsner dates Welwick House 1690, and the earliest local record is 1726, the date of its acquisition by Thomas Pierson. The paper is stamped on the back with an unusual excise stamp and the number 127, possibly dating it 1714.
Norfolk Museums Service (Kings Lynn Museums).

On following pages
Colour 4 *Left*
English wallpaper, early eighteenth century, from a house in Colchester, Essex. Block printed and stencilled.
Victoria and Albert Museum, London
25 *Right*
Wall decoration of alternating panels of flock paper and embossed leather from Ivy House, Worcester, English, *c.*1679.
Victoria and Albert Museum, London.

printed wallpaper, probably from *indiennes* (the name given to decorated cottons, stencilled or coloured freehand by brush, that were originally imported from India by the trading companies). *Indiennes* were used at first as hangings and bedcovers, and later as clothing. Their bright, fast colours and exotic chintz patterns made them extremely popular and precipitated an increase in the interest and skill devoted to the production of floral patterns in both England and France.

Indiennes were used as a wallcovering at Versailles in 1580, and countless imitations followed. When in 1686 Louis XIV prohibited their importation and manufacture in France, he incidentally gave a boost to the progress of wallpaper. Manufacturers were forced to do other kinds of work, and many began to turn out printed and painted papers in designs that were much influenced by printed fabrics. This generally meant that the colours as well as the outlines were printed now, and since the sheets of paper were stuck together before printing, the woodblocks, and therefore the designs too, could be larger, to give an effect of far greater continuity and coherence.

To some extent these innovations were due to Jean Papillon (1661-1723)

42

and his son Jean Michel (1698-1776). Papillon Senior is regarded by many as the true father of wallpaper, such was his impact on both production techniques and styles. In 1688 he took over his father's printing house for wallpapers, using very large woodblocks and drawing direct on to them, to produce the first all-over repeating and continuous designs. It was his son who was to make the greater mark on the history of wallpaper, however. At the age of nine he cut his first woodblock after a design by his father and the finished article was shown in their collection in 1707. Later he wrote a historical and practical dissertation on the art of woodblock engraving. He worked on all aspects of wallpaper production and hanging and contributed notes on the subject to the writer Diderot for his massive encyclopaedia. Unfortunately, Papillon's notes and his excellent illustration were dropped, as Diderot, it seems, finally considered wallpaper too insignificant a topic to merit more than a brief summary.

During the seventeenth century, too, the importation of Chinese and Japanese papers was making a remarkable impact. It was at this time that the Dutch, French and English East India companies, whose enormous power and exotic aura can hardly be appreciated today, began their trading activities, mostly in tea. The Chinese seem to have been reluctant to have anything to do with Europeans, and neither they nor the Japanese were very impressed with the goods offered in exchange. When they did agree to trade, they insisted on being paid largely in silver. Although Elizabeth I sent two letters to the Emperor of China, apparently neither reached him. Portugal succeeded in establishing a depot at Macao on the Chinese coast, but it was Holland who had the first successful trade arrangements. Britain did not really start dealing until 1690, although tea (or 'ch'a') had been sold at a London coffee house as early as 1657. The first Chinese wallpapers were certainly sold at the famous tea centres, but it is unclear whether they were used as packing in the tea chests or were included as a commercial experiment. An early piece of documentation, noted by E. A. Entwisle in *The Connoisseur,* June 1934, records an auction sale held in Birchin Lane, London, in 1695, of various lots of paper, one of which was listed as 66½ 'pieces of Japan paper for hangings', by which is probably meant Chinese paper. Unfortunately the list bears no indication of the value of the goods.

The Chinese wallpapers met with an enormous success. Their intimacy, originality and quiet gaiety appealed strongly to the emerging merchant class, as well as to the more aristocratic. The designs seem to have fallen into three main groups: landscapes; birds and flowers, intermingled with insects, especially grasshoppers and butterflies; and scenes of domestic life. The draughtsmanship was excellent and the colours were beautiful, bright and long-lasting. But the main secret behind the success of these papers was a rare combination of informality and grandeur which made them suitable for a great variety of houses.

Opinions seem divided as to whether the papers were actually used in

28
A print from the block engraved by Jean Michel Papillon at the age of nine, in 1707.
Bibliothèque Nationale, Paris.

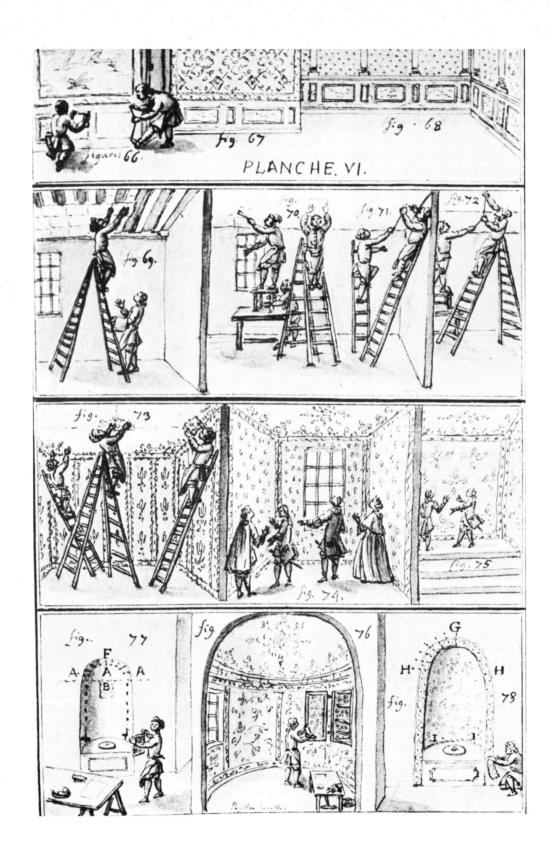

PLANCHE. VI.

figures 66.   fig. 67.   fig. 68.

fig. 69.   fig. 70.   fig. 71.   fig. 72.

fig. 73.   fig. 74.   fig. 75.

fig. 77.   fig. 76.   fig. 78.

China itself. The Chinese seem generally to have preferred a more changeable decoration, with more clear spaces. In any case, as their designs were quickly adapted to meet the demands of a western public, compromises were made in the characteristic subtleties which went unappreciated by occidental eyes. It is only fair to say, however, that an aesthetic, and not merely commercial, impact may have been felt from Europe. There is an example in the Victoria and Albert Museum, London, of a Cantonese wallpaper which has been heavily influenced by the French painter Watteau, and although this is of a later period, it seems quite possible that there may have been an exchange of ideas, however slight, much earlier than this.

The Chinese papers were very costly and fragile. European manufacturers soon set to work on copies, particularly in the Low Countries, Flanders and Germany. An example of an early eighteenth-century wallpaper showing an oriental influence (in this case more a loosely stylistic borrowing than a slavish imitation), and combining it with the popular technique of flock work, is the paper from Hurlcote Manor already mentioned (see Plate 26). What it most obviously lacks is an understanding of the oriental designers' use of space, a failing which seems to have been common to both the European imitators and their public. The European *horror vacui* is well illustrated by the following quotation of 1738, an order from Thomas Hancock of Boston to Thomas Rowe, stationer of London. He encloses a sample of wallpaper, which is

> all that is left of a Room Lately Come over here, and takes much in the Town and will be the only paper-hanging for sale wh. am of opinion may answer very well. Therefore desire you by all means to get mine well Done and as Cheap as Possible, and if they can make it more beautiful by adding more Birds flying here and there, with some Landskips at the Bottom, Should like it well. Let the ground be of the same colour as the pattern. At The Top and Bottom was a narrow Border of about 2″ wide. wh. [I] would have to mine. About three or four years ago, my friend Francis Wilks, Esq. had a Hanging done in the Same manner but much handsomer, Sent over here by Mr. Sam Waldon of this place, made by one Dunbar, in Aldermanbury, where no doubt he or some of his successors may be found. In other parts of this Hangings [sic] are a Great Variety of Different Sorts of Birds, Peacocks, Macoys, Squirril, Monkys, Fruit and Flowers, &c*

The imitations varied enormously. Some were very improbable—a grotesque mixture of European and oriental cultures, clothes and landscapes. It was this element of the grotesque and the crudity of the imitations which eventually led to the waning of the vogue, although it never died completely. It survives today both in the form of actual hand-painted Chinese papers and in the continuing general influence on European designs. In the United States, moreover, there has always seemed to be a particular penchant for Chinese wallpaper. Several

30
Anonymous English wallpaper showing a Chinese influence, unused, from Ord House,
Berwick-on-Tweed. Wood block printed, colours added by stencil, *c.*1700.

Victoria and Albert Museum, London.

29 Opposite
Illustration of hanging wallpaper by Jean Michel Papillon, 1730–40.
Deutsches Tapetenmuseum, Kassel.

* Quoted from C. C. Oman 'English Chinoiserie Wallpapers' *Country Life* 11 February 1933

American firms still specialize in careful handpainted copies of Chinese
originals. Most of the examples that survive are from the eighteenth
century, when the vogue was revitalized, and these will be dealt with in
more detail in a later chapter. One point that should be mentioned now,
however, is the confusion between 'Chinese', 'Indian' and 'Japan'
wallpapers: the terms were interchangeable. Although trading was
certainly carried out with these countries, and though Indian woven and
painted materials were imported, there are no wallpapers which are known
to be specifically either Indian or Japanese. The difficulty is rather akin to
that which arises because the term *papiers peints* (the French for wallpaper,
be it printed or painted) has been too literally translated into English as
painted paper, regardless of the methods employed. But whatever its
precise make-up, the oriental influence described here, combined with the

46

work of the Papillons, was greatly effective in stimulating the demand for wallpaper. So rapidly did the market expand that, as Savary des Bruslons remarked in his *Dictionary* of 1723, by the end of the seventeenth century there was hardly a house in Paris that could not boast of some *papiers peints*.

The Pioneering Spirit

THE eighteenth century was a period of expansion and growth, with European communities becoming more suburban and more wealthy. International trade became better organized, and settlers in newly colonized countries began to find their feet. Although wallpaper continued to compete with all the more traditional types of wall covering and to some extent to imitate them, it gradually came to be appreciated too in its own right, and as less of a novelty than hitherto. It is recorded by William Pyne, the historian for Kensington Palace, that Kent, the Palace architect, decorated the King's Great Drawing Room with wallpaper, to the surprise and admiration of George I.

Although paperstaining (as the wallpaper business was frequently called at the time) gained ground in the seventeenth century, it did not become widespread or widely documented until the eighteenth century. It seems that a little before 1700, the largest group of wallpaper makers in not only England but Europe were gathered in the East End of London, around St Paul's churchyard. They were not all, by any means, concerned only with wallpaper; in the same place the allied skills of older crafts were practised, including printing, leather gilding and the making of playing cards. The versatility of these craftsmen is remarkable. Matthias Darly, the wallpaper maker, was also responsible for many of the illustrations in Chippendale's ambitious and unique *Director,* first published in 1754 with 160 engraved plates. The third edition, issued in 1762 with an increased number of illustrations, actually included designs for paper hangings, an item that indicated Chippendale's increasing interest in interior decoration. Conversely, Darly himself had already brought out a book of designs for chairs. His trade card in the Banks Collection at the British Museum explains that he could produce work

> Neatly fitted up either with Paintings or Stainings in the Modern, Gothic, or Chinese Tastes for Town or Country; & large Allowance for Ready Money. N.B. Paper for Exportation and Sketches or Designs for Gentlemen's Different Fancies. Letters post paid Duly Answered. Engraving in all its Branches, viz.: Visiting Tickets, Coats of Arms, Seals, Book Plates, Frontispieces, Shopkeeper's Bills, &c., in Greater Variety and Cheaper than at any other Shop in Town.

Eventually wallpaper production became the most prominent activity carried out in this area. The names of specific designers have not come down to us, but many of the names of the manufacturers survive in directories of the time, and on their trade cards. These cards often have elaborate designs of excellent workmanship, and are very finely detailed. They give some clue to the style of the products which they advertise and in some cases an insight into the establishments they come from.

One of the most well-known of these factories was the Blew Paper Warehouse, whose name may refer to the flock papers probably produced there. The colour blue, which has always been used in country cottages to discourage flies, played a particularly important role in interior decoration at the time. It was widely used for paper hangings, especially flock, and flock papers, particularly abroad, were widely known as 'Blew papers'. Blue walls were perhaps favoured because they set off to great advantage the richly figured mahogany employed in the furniture of the time. But the popularity of the colour had also a less obvious cause. To protect the wool and silk trades in England, an act was passed in 1700 forbidding the importation of Indian silks and printed calicoes for use in either dress or furnishings, and this prohibition was extended in 1720 to all painted, printed, stained or dyed calicoes, whether imported or home-manufactured. Although this act was later repealed when the importance of the cotton industry became apparent, there was a period when only 'single colour blue' linen was allowed to be produced in England. It escaped the embargo because of the antiquity of its production. There was at the same time a vogue for matching wallpapers and furniture coverings, and since there must have been more blue material available than anything else, the predominance of blue was strengthened.

The use of blue in this way is mentioned in many letters and diaries of the time. Chippendale, whose role as an interior decorator seems to have been underestimated, used blue verditer papers on the chimney boards at Nostell Priory, Yorkshire, where he was also commissioned to procure 'Indian' paper for three rooms and to supervise its hanging, as well as attend to the curtains, blinds and borders. Horace Walpole also used plain blue wallpaper in conjunction with a chintz bedcover, and in another room printed his blue paper and linen from the same block, a practice which has recently returned to favour.

Another whose work was reputed to be very fine was Thomas Bromwich, of the Golden Lyon, Ludgate Hill. Again it was a firm which, like the Blew Paper Warehouse, continued with various partners from about 1700 to the middle of the nineteenth century. Walpole chiefly relied on the papers of this family business. It seems to have been quite famous, and produced work of a particularly high quality, although Walpole had occasion to complain about the prices when, having been let down by his friend Bentley who had promised to paint up a gothic paper for him, he was compelled instead 'to give Bromwich's man God knows what to do it'. Bromwich is also mentioned in the diaries of Mrs Phillip Lybbe Powys. After a visit to Mrs Freeman's at Fawley Court, Buckinghamshire, in October 1771, Mrs Powys describes the decor:

> On the left hand of the saloon is a large billiard room hung with the most beautiful pink India paper, adorn'd with very good prints, the borders cut out and the ornaments put on with great taste by Bromwich.
>
> The dressing room to this is prettier than tis possible to imagine, the most curious India paper has birds, flowers, etc. put up as different pictures in frames of the same, with festoons, India baskets, figures, etc. on a pea green paper, Mr Bromwich having again display'd his taste as in

the billiard room below and both having an effect wonderfully pleasing.*

Wallpaper manufacturers of this period doubled as retailers, and would also advise on decorative schemes and supervise their execution. The manufacturer was often called upon to be a complete interior designer and decorator, choosing upholstery and other textiles to accompany his own wallpapers. A German engraving entitled *The Paper Hanger at Work,* dating from about 1790, depicts what must have been a relatively common scene in the houses of the well-to-do in Europe and, to a lesser extent, in America. In the illustration, the workman is using nails for pinning the wallpaper to the walls. This was quite a common practice, though in an English bill of the time a customer was charged both for 'tacks and glew'. The method of hanging wallpaper apparently varied not only from house to house and from manufacturer to manufacturer, but from section to section of the same wall. The day of the separate wallpaper hanger and, of course, of the amateur decorator, was far in the future. The successful hanging of wallpaper was at that time a much more risky business: colours were not reliably fast, so that any glue spilled on the face of the paper was likely to smear as well as stain.

The way in which the talents of wallpaper makers were widely stretched to include a multitude of jobs is illustrated by several bills for Bromwich's work which came into the possession of E. A. Entwisle during the first half of this century. One proclaims that Bromwich makes and sells 'all manner of Screens, Window Blinds, and Covers for Tables, Rooms, Cabins, Stair-Cases, etc. Hung with Guilt Leather, or India Pictures, Chints's, Callicoes, Cottons, Needlework and Damasks Matched in Paper to the utmost exactness, at Reasonable Rates.' In addition to this commendable list of skills, there is an account on the reverse of the bill for lining a 'Baby House' with various fine papers.

Another firm which won praise along with Bromwich, was that of Crompton and Spinnage, who were in business in 1740 and possibly before, and continued until 1772. They were suppliers to the Royal Household, and were patronized by the aristocracy. Like Bromwich, they also produced papier mâché decorations.

There were others of whom less is known but whose names, addresses and sometimes products survive. Traces of many more have probably vanished. Among those that have survived are John Hutton at the Golden Lyon, St Paul's Churchyard, who was succeeded by his nephew William Barbaroux; and Joseph Fletcher at the King's Arms, St Paul's Churchyard, whose business was taken over by John Conway. Both of these apparently worked mostly in gilded leather, a medium which still continued to be a serious rival of paper hangings. Robert Halford and John Scott also worked on leather and paper in London at this time. James Minnikin specialized more in paper, and so did Edward Butling at the Old Knave of Clubs, Southwark Bridge, one of the few of this group who was primarily

* Quoted from E. A. Entwisle 'Bromwich of Ludgate Hill', *Journal of Decorative Art* November 1941

51

33
The Paper Hanger at Work, an
engraving *c.* 1790.
   Deutsches Tapetenmuseum, Kassel.

a stationer. John Seagood, bookseller; John Hall; Salt and Baker; Samuel Smith; Robert Stark; James Wheeley; Nathaniel Taylor; Tootle and Young; Buzzard—these are the names of some of the men involved in the manufacture and retailing of wallpaper at whose styles and lives one can only hazard a guess. Their advertisements are the sole clue. The only certainty is that there was an enormous variety in their products, although one dominant trend was a taste for chinoiserie in a very anglicized form.

One figure who stands out from the rest is John Baptist Jackson, whose papers Robert Dunbar used to sell when he was in business in Aldermanbury in 1720. Jackson is one of the more memorable characters in the history of wallpaper, perhaps largely by chance rather than by merit. There is considerable documentation of his activities, and the information we have has a rather individual air about it. He was born in 1701, was eventually apprenticed to an engraver called Kirkall, but in 1726 went to Paris where he worked for Jean Michel Papillon. Papillon maintained that he employed him out of pity, but this turned out to be misplaced. Jackson tried to make extra copies of designs and sell them on the side, and since Papillon was not impressed with his efficiency either, he lost his job and was forced to hawk his own engravings round printing offices in Paris. Despite some success, he was soon obliged to leave Paris, travelling through France and visiting Rome and Venice, where he took a wife. He copied many masterpieces there, and his engravings were reproduced in Italy. On his return to England, however, he had to turn his experience to the production of wallpaper (for there was no demand for his fine art engravings), and he opened a factory at Battersea in 1746. In 1754 he issued a booklet laying claim to the invention of chiaroscuro printing in wallpapers and the use of oil colours. This publication was an essay in self-advertisement, though in fairness one should say that the boastful style was a typical feature of writing at the time. Reproachfully, the booklet looked back to the lack of interest and patronage that Jackson had received in England.

Jackson's general method was to produce not repeating patterns but pictures to be spaced widely over the wall area or contained within printed frames. His colours were often heavy and sticky looking, his relief effects bold. Horace Walpole remarked that his Venetian prints were objectionable in their aspiration to be copies of Titian (or, as in the example illustrated here, Tintoretto), but if one allowed them to be barbarous bas reliefs, they succeeded to a miraculous degree. Eventually he succumbed to barbarism and used them at Strawberry Hill.

In eighteenth-century England the makers of paper hangings undeniably prospered and multiplied, to a degree that was surprising in view of the major obstacle they had to overcome. This obstacle was a tax, initiated in 1712, imposed on 'printed, painted or stained' paper. In 1712 it was levied at a rate of 1d. per square yard, in the following year the rate was 1½d., and subsequently it rose to 1¾d. The stamping of papers by excise

34
The first page of a booklet issued by John Baptist Jackson in 1754.
British Museum, London.

53

36
Wallpaper formerly attributed to
John Baptist Jackson from
Doddington Hall, Lincs, mid-
eighteenth century.
Victoria and Albert Museum,
London.

officials, however, did not begin until 2 August 1714. Although Queen
Anne died on 7 August of that year, there must have been a brief period
when stamps bearing her device were used, before the manufacture and
delivery of new ones. The flock paper found at Welwick House, South
Lynn (Plate 24), bears several examples of an excise duty stamp with a royal
coat of arms unlike that of the Georgian stamps. Whether or not it relates
to Queen Anne, which seems likely, is impossible to say for sure, since all
the stamps are too indistinct for positive identification. No other definite
examples from this period have been discovered, most existing stamps

35 *Opposite*
An example of Jackson's 'Venetian
Prints'—*The Crucifixion after
Tintoretto,* published 1745.
Whitworth Art Gallery,
University of Manchester.

Various Excise Duty Stamps.

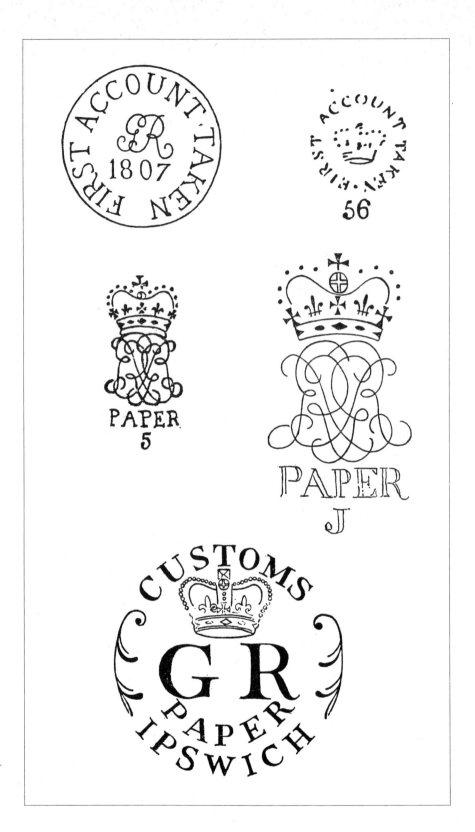

bearing the monogram 'G.R.', which was used in a period unhelpfully stretching from 1714 to 1830.

In an attempt to stop evasion of duty and the counterfeiting of stamps, preliminary marking of blank paper was enforced in 1716, and later, to close another loop hole, another stamp was introduced: the 'Duty Charged Remnant' stamp. Moreover, each maker of paper hangings was obliged from 1784 to buy a licence costing £4 a year to help pay for the American War of Independence. These levies, burden enough in themselves, were made more irritating by the difficult process of their enforcement. Each sheet of paper, whether printed or painted, had to be stamped at both ends by an excise officer, so that the crafty workmen could not add extra pieces afterwards. One story claims that a manufacturer produced a whole room's worth of paper after the excise officer had gone home, took it to the site and trimmed it to length, carefully destroying the place where the tax stamps would have been. The whole stamping procedure now seems a joyless and self-defeating piece of bureaucracy. Throughout the century regulations on this matter were continually being revised, sometimes to the mystification of the officials involved and to the aggrievement of the manufacturers. The latter continued to thrive, but their prices and profits cannot have failed to be affected. Offenders were strictly dealt with. In 1773 the death penalty was introduced for forging stamps, although in Ireland the punishment was merely a £500 fine or transportation for seven years; and in 1773 also, a duty was imposed on imported papers, which may have somewhat facilitated the selling of English papers at home. Because of the Napoleonic Wars, the rates on home-produced paper were raised to 9d. a square yard in 1803, and in 1809 they were increased to 1s. for as long as the war lasted and for another six months besides. In the event, the shilling rate was retained until 1847, when the tax was reduced to 2d. It was finally abandoned in 1861.

French manufacturers worked under easier circumstances. Indeed, they were encouraged to employ good artists and an import duty on foreign papers must have aided home production. Nevertheless, even in France, English papers made great headway, and Mme de Pompadour used them for her dressing room at Versailles and a bathroom at Chateau Champs. Despite the higher prices of English wallpaper, it continued to outsell its French competitors. This was partly because the multifarious work of the *dominotiers,* which had always been much more of a force to be reckoned with in Europe, survived in France and the neighbouring countries and absorbed much of the interest and talent which might otherwise have been channelled into wallpaper. As a result of this, the effects in France of Papillon's pioneering work in the continuity of designs for wallhangings were somewhat delayed. The limitations of *dominotier* work proved difficult to break out of, but before long the inevitable departure occurred. De Fourcroy, working in Paris at the beginning of the eighteenth century, although a *cartier-dominotier,* did produce some wallpapers strongly

influenced by Papillon. The names of many others survive, but little of
their work. As in England, the businesses of this time can be traced
through from their founders to sons, nephews and widows, but new firms
also sprang up, started by apprentices who left their employers to establish
businesses of their own.

   One of the anonymous French products of this period, a set of five
panels in the Chinese style, shows the continuing strength of the taste for
oriental decoration, and makes an interesting comparison with the German
example of about the same period (Colour Plate 5). They are different in
design yet both of them bear witness to the widespread interest in
chinoiserie wallpapers in Europe. English papers were no less popular,
however. Some of the French manufacturers advertised themselves as
producing papers in the English manner. One, Didier Aubert, son-in-law
of Papillon, is named in the *Journal Oeconomique* of March 1755 as the
only producer in France of flock wallpapers, turning out work that is 'just
as beautiful and just as perfect as English papers' in one or more colours,
and designing them in the style of the most beautiful damasks. His
establishment, like that of numerous merchants who made and sold
pictures, cards and book endpapers, was originally situated in the rue
Saint-Jacques. Much later, in the nineteenth century, another Aubert,
whose first name was Charles, worked as the pupil of Owen Jones, the
notable designer. The name Aubert in fact crops up on several occasions
in the history of wallpaper; this is probably simply coincidence, but may

40
Wallpaper produced by the
Remondini family active in Bassano,
Italy during the eighteenth century,
very much in the *dominotier* tradition.
Museo Civico di Bassano del Grappa.

41
Another wallpaper produced by the
Remondini family.
Museo Civico di Bassano del Grappa.

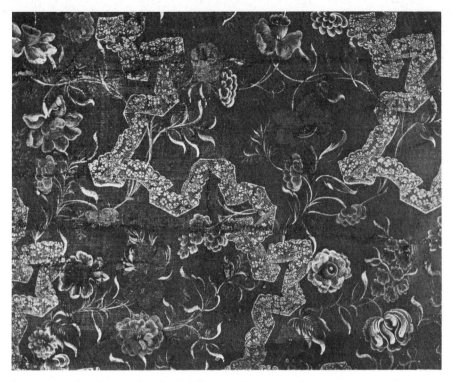

42
Wachstuchtapete produced by
Nothnagel in Frankfurt, *c.* 1760.
Deutsches Tapetenmuseum.

be yet another instance of a family continuing in the same business.

In many other European communities, home production of wallpaper plagiarized the styles of England and France, or alternatively, imports from those countries were sold instead. The widow of a wallpaper maker in Ireland, petitioning Parliament in 1763, said that in order to maintain her standards she 'supplied herself constantly with the newest patterns in the English and Indian strain and provided herself with Journeymen from abroad and Apprentices instructed at home.'* In Ireland, production of paper hangings was often incorporated with house painting as a single composite job, done by one firm.

In Italy, throughout the eighteenth century, there was one particularly famous family which worked with wallpaper, the Remondinis. They produced fine art prints, for which there was far more of a market in Italy than elsewhere, as John Baptist Jackson had found to his cost. They also made prints which were far more squarely in the tradition of purely decorative wallpaper, and these tended to have a very pleasing directness and simple boldness of style.

In Germany, wallpaper had one particularly popular competitor, and that was a special sort of linen, called *Wachstuchtapete,* primed, stencilled and printed in oil colours. Goethe describes its production at the factory of J. A. B. Nothnagel, painter and etcher of Frankfurt, in the fourth book of *Dichtung und Wahrheit.* The bonding material used in the manufacture of printed linen contained wax, which helped to keep the base supple for

* Quoted from Ada K. Longfield 'History of the Dublin Wallpaper Industry'
Journal of the Royal Society of Antiquities of Ireland LXXVII, ii, 1947, pp.101ff

43
'Herrnhuter Kleister-Papier', *c.* 1770,
produced by means of a wooden comb
and fingers in the same way as
imitation wood graining. These were
special products of Böhmischen
Brüder Gemeinde, established in the
small town of Herrnhut, Saxony, in
1722. The firm continued until *c.* 1825.
Deutsches Tapetenmuseum, Kassel.

longer, and the pieces were painted with a layer of varnish to make them
washable, a convenience which makers of wallcoverings have always been
eager to develop. The popularity of printed linen hangings, as well as
painted ones, eclipsed and possibly even stunted the growth of the
wallpaper vogue in Germany. There is less surviving material relating to
the development of wallpaper in Germany than there is elsewhere in
Europe, and the inevitable conclusion is that its development there lagged
behind the well-documented boom in England and France. However,
isolated examples of eighteenth-century German paper decoration have
been found, and there was a paper mill in Augsberg as early as 1389.

It is at this point that America enters our story. For the first forty years,
the life of the colonists was too arduous for decoration to figure much in
their thoughts. There were no luxuries until the end of the seventeenth
century. Walls remained whitewashed or painted with clay and water.
Soon, however, brighter colours were used and borders painted by
amateurs were added. Sometimes chimney breasts or even whole rooms
were painted with landscapes and romantic scenes. It was not until the
second quarter of the eighteenth century that wallpapers came into the
country, and when they did it was at first only through individuals
ordering them specially from London or Paris. By 1745, however,
wallpaper was being retailed in America. Charles Hargreave of Philadelphia advertised it in that year, and it soon gained great popularity.

In 1765 the first American factory was set up by John Rugar in New York. Another factory was started in Boston in the 1780s by John Walsh, and although he went bankrupt, the firm continued under the ownership of Moses Grant. Simultaneously, Joseph Hovey was printing papers and linens in Boston. In the same town the firm of Prentis and May was established, and later the partners split up to make two separate concerns. Wallpaper businesses all over the country were multiplying. Peter Fleeson, sometimes known as Plunkett Heeson, set up a business in Philadelphia; and in 1790, Boulu and Carden, the first wallpaper firm of any great size, began producing in association with John Carnes, who had earlier been the American consul in Lyons. Meanwhile, the firm of John Howell and Son transferred their business from England to Albany, and the enterprise continued well into the twentieth century.

Here again, as might be expected, the influence of England and France reigned supreme, since papers from these countries were bought and copied not only for stylistic, fashionable and possibly snobbish reasons, but also because they had the added virtue of stemming from what many Americans must still have regarded as home.

In all the wallpapers produced at this time, no matter what their country of origin, there was a greater liveliness of style than there had been before, a lightening of colour and a relaxing of the symmetry and formality of earlier designs. The bright floral design that dominates most people's ideas about wallpaper was coming into its own. This new restrained gaiety can perhaps be attributed to several causes: the influence of Chinese papers and *indiennes* imported by the East India companies; the contemporary European taste for the Rococo; the growing confidence and skill of designers of wallpaper; and the bright optimism of the economically expanding countries that were busily manufacturing it. For the same reasons, it was a time also of growing inventiveness, imagination and variety, qualities that are very well exemplified in the various styles of wallpaper used to decorate Walpole's house at Strawberry Hill, as described in a letter Walpole wrote to Sir Horace Mann in 1753:

> Now you shall walk into the house; the bow window leads into a little parlour hung with some coloured Gothic paper and Jackson's Venetian prints; from hence you come to the hall and staircase; imagine the walls covered with (I call it paper painted in perspective to represent) Gothic fretwork . . . the room on the ground floor nearest you is a bedchamber hung with yellow paper and prints framed in the manner invented by Lord Cadogan, with black and white borders printed . . . [the closet] is hung with green paper and watercolour pictures; out of this closet is the room where we always live, hung with a blue and white paper adorned with festoons and a thousand plump chairs and couches, and luxurious settees covered with linen of the same pattern. Underneath this room is a cool little hall, where we generally dine, hung with paper to imitate Dutch tiles.

An Age of Gentility

WHATEVER their specialized interests, chroniclers of taste who choose the whole of the western world as their province, or even merely two or three countries, face difficulties when it comes to labelling periods. Such are the historical differences and time lags in artistic development from one country to another, that it is hard to speak of an 'era' without simplifying complexities and rounding off contradictions. Thus, my Age of Gentility must accommodate the violence of the French Revolution and the hardships of the American settlers. Being English, I am tempted to use terms like Regency and Georgian, but this would be too insular. Being European, I am tempted to use words like Rococo, but in fact much of the wallpaper of the time is not particularly of this style. The quality that best indicates the aesthetic temper of the age, at least in so far as it is reflected in wallpaper, is perhaps, after all, gentility. From the late eighteenth century until the beginning of the machine age, wallpapers were predominantly genteel; at their best they were designed with restraint and a large measure of good taste.

That is not to say there were not elements which would today be found fussy. A particular example is the widespread use of papier mâché, a material which attained great popularity and an enormous variety of applications. Intended as a cheap imitation of plaster work, this material, made from pulped paper, whiting and glue, was moulded and grew harder and stronger as it matured. A great deal of experience must have been employed in its production, for it is indistinguishable from the old skilled plaster work which it emulated, and its mouldings and ornaments are often delicate. It was largely an English development, and although it continued well into the nineteenth century, machines producing heavily embossed paper eventually took over the market for which papier mâché catered.

Although paper continued to be hand-made in small sheets which varied in size from country to country, during the middle of the eighteenth century the practice of sticking sheets together before printing to form a roll became common. In England the standard length of a 'piece' (a term still used in the wallpaper industry for a roll) was established by the excise officials as twelve yards.

In the printing process itself, the traditional wood blocks were still

manipulated by hand, and still made of pear or sycamore nailed down to a
pine backing. Thick lines and masses were in wood, while fine lines were in
copper which had been driven into the wood, for isolated raised wooden
edges could not stand the very great pressure incurred during printing or
the continual washing that was necessary. The face of the block had to be
kept as even as possible to ensure good printing, and this was a continual
problem since wood swells when damp and copper, of course, does not.

There is a description of hand-block printing in the notebooks of
Metford Warner which to some degree explains the painting of a wallpaper
maker's workshop, by an unknown Hull artist, illustrated in Plate 45.
Each printer had a printing table with a press consisting of a flat bed on
which the paper was laid and a vertical pole immediately above it, which,
by means of a treadle worked by the foot, swung down to bring just the
desired pressure on the printing block. At the side of the table stood a

trough of paper pulp or something similarly viscid, over which rested a lightly stretched cloth, making an elastic bed. On this was placed a trough made of another tightly stretched cloth on which the colour was spread and on which the block, having been removed from the press for a moment, was pressed downwards by hand. The printer then took the inked block back to the press, and controlling it by a strap fixed to its back, brought it down on to the paper, manipulating the pole down after it by means of the treadle. Different patterns required more or less pressure. Two or more colours could be printed at the same time if they were sufficiently far apart. The blocks used were usually twenty-one inches wide, although the length varied from twenty-one inches down to as little as ten. In hand block printing, unlike the industrial printing that was of a later date, the blocks could be turned in different directions to give the impression of a much larger design.

In the second half of the eighteenth century, hand printing reached a peak, and newly refined skills in this field led to another interesting new development in the history of wallpaper: the phenomenon of the print room. In rooms specially set aside for the purpose, fine art prints of excellent quality would be pasted directly on to the walls and framed by paper borders. The idea has been attributed to Lord Cardigan and it is certain that one of the notable exponents of it was Chippendale. Despite the proximity and variety of the prints and their ornate frames, often planned and put in position in person by the owners of the houses where they are to be found, the result appears to have been calm and sedate. Again it seems to have been a British innovation. The idea was apparently sometimes copied in contemporary decorative painting. On the staircase at Hickstead Place, Bolney, Sussex, for instance, is a scheme which looks very much at first glance like a print room, but is in fact painted, and in the long gallery at Castletown, County Kildare, was a display very similar to the Pompeian style of its print room, but in reality painted on directly by an Irish artist named Thomas Riley. In both schemes at Castletown, copies of portraits by Reynolds of one of the ladies of the house have been incorporated. One person who was immensely pleased by this new trend was the luckless John Baptist Jackson, whose prints at last found a potential market.

46
The Print Room at Castletown House, Co. Kildare. Prints were being collected for it as early as 1762.
Bord Failte.

It was doubtless still the case at this time that the manufacturer was usually in charge of the hanging of the paper, though in some cases it would have been the responsibility of the person who organized the whole decorative scheme—the furniture maker, for instance, whose task it often was to solve all the practical and aesthetic problems involved. With print rooms, however, one feels that there was much more participation from the members of the household, both in the choice and arrangement of the various scenes. Methods of hanging wallpaper still varied; although direct pasting had been used for well over a hundred years, nailing was still in some favour, and the more costly papers were still backed with canvas and stretched over battens.

These more expensive papers were largely Chinese ones, for which there was a renewed vogue. England retains a wealth of beautiful examples of this second blossoming. Sets of Chinese wallpaper usually comprised twenty-five sheets of handpainted paper, four feet wide and twelve feet long. The designs seem bolder and the colours more vivid than those first imported to the west. A good example of this fashion is to be found in the Saloon at Brighton Pavilion. It shows the most popular type of design: birds, foliage and butterflies, all exquisitely drawn, with a decorative balustrade and plant pots at the base. The background is yellow, which is slightly unusual, green or blue being the common preference. The design also incorporates the panelling which was a relatively common device at this time, borders for framing, as we have seen, being part of the stock-in-trade of wallpaper manufacturers. In about 1820, the original Chinese wallpaper was removed from the Saloon to make way for a new painted decoration bearing a resemblance to crimson damask hangings. The present paper, very similar to the original shown in contemporary illustrations, was given in 1856 by Queen Victoria.

Another well-known example occurs in the Chinese Drawing Room at Temple Newsam House, Leeds (Colour Plate 7). It is very similar to the paper at Brighton Pavilion, which is not surprising, since both papers are said to have been bought originally by the Prince Regent from Crace and Son in 1802. The Prince, seeing Lady Hertford at a race meeting, fancied that he was in love with her, and on 28 September 1806 he paid a morning visit to Temple Newsam House, her home, and presented the young lady's mother with several rolls of wallpaper. The walls of the room which was to be its final destination had only just been re-covered with a block-printed paper, and in any case the exotic gift was probably not quite to the mother's rather restrained taste. However, family tradition maintains that the paper was hung in the 1820s, possibly as a sentimental tribute to the prince who had been Lady Hertford's companion.

The design is on a green ground, divided into panels edged with a strip of silver papier mâché in imitation of Chinese fretwork. Interestingly, the previous paper, an oak leaf garland, shows quite clearly through the striped areas that surround the Chinese paper panels. Lady Hertford found the

68

47
A Chinese wallpaper given by Queen
Victoria in 1856, but probably older,
closely resembling the original
wallpaper used in the first scheme, in
the Saloon, Brighton Pavilion.
Brighton Corporation.

spaciousness of the oriental design rather bleak, so like many of her
contemporaries she decorated the more empty places with extra motifs
from the surplus fragments of paper, in some cases removing pieces from
areas of the wallpaper that had been hung in a dark corner, in order to show
them off to greater advantage. This, however, was still not enough, and she
proceeded to add birds from ornithological plates. The source of these was
recently discovered by Mr Waldemar H. Fries to be John James
Audubon's classic series 'The Birds of America', the original edition of
which was published in London between 1827 and 1838. The plates were
hand-coloured aquatint engravings printed on double elephant folio
sheets. The series was issued to subscribers in eighty-seven parts of five
plates each, but Lady Hertford apparently defaulted after receiving the
first volume of a hundred plates. She dismembered only ten of them,
however, which gave her twenty-five birds in all. The American birds
blend remarkably well with their Chinese neighbours. They tend to be
placed over the joins between the rolls of the Chinese paper, or in groups
on panels over the doors.

There are other excellent examples of Chinese work to be seen in
England, especially at Chatsworth House, Derbyshire, Nostell Priory,
Yorkshire, and the Victoria and Albert Museum. Although they all follow
approximately the same pattern, featuring all sorts of brilliantly coloured
birds among luxuriant foliage, since they are all handpainted, no two are
identical.

51
Late eighteenth century Chinese
wallpaper, brought to England by
Lord Macartney. From the Board
Room of Coutts Bank.
By courtesy of Messrs. Coutts
and Co., London.

Colour 5 *Opposite above*
South German wallpaper, c. 1729,
showing oriental influence. Once in
the possession of a noble of the Holy
Roman Empire.
Albgaumuseum, Ettlingen.

Colour 6 *Opposite below*
English chinoiserie panels, c. 1770.
Printed from an etched plate and
coloured by hand and stencilled.
Whitworth Art Gallery,
University of Manchester.

Another style of wallpaper of this period was brought back in 1794 by
Lord Macartney (who had been to China to negotiate commercial treaties
there) and was used to decorate Coutts Bank, London. It is a figurative
paper showing scenes of daily life, and its rich and brilliant colours create
an impressive picture of some of the principal Chinese trades and
occupations and mythical episodes. Against a background of deep cream
and a naturalistically coloured landscape, many brightly coloured figures
go about their work. The scenes include a potter at his wheel, drying and
firing processes and the carrying away of the finished pots in a junk. Other
vignettes are the gathering and stacking of rice; a representation of a
petitioner and judge; stages in silk production and the growing of tea;
gardening; and an outdoor playhouse with actors and actresses:

In other countries than England the Chinese vogue was more commonly
a matter of copying oriental styles than of direct importation. Westernized
versions of oriental types of design were produced in France and
Germany, and Beckmann, in his *History of Inventions,* 1797, refers to a
'kind of Chinese paper' he once saw in Petersburg. England did contribute
to this aspect of the fashion too, however, although no names survive, and
America, meanwhile, was eagerly importing chinoiserie designs from

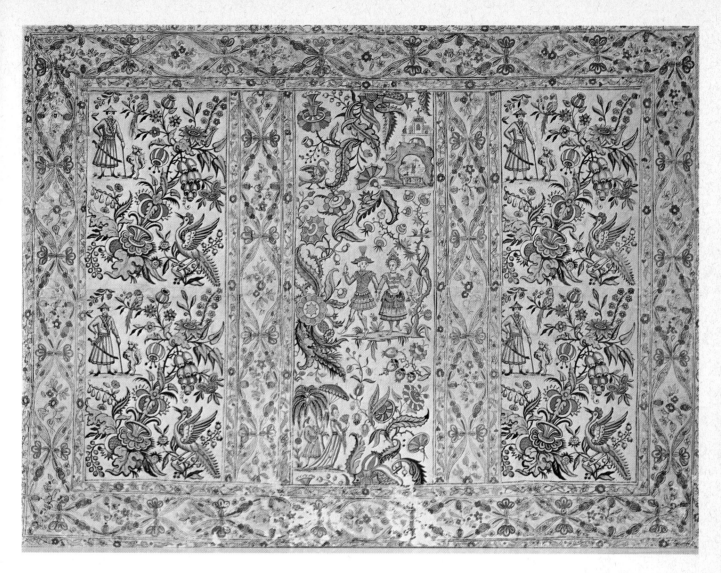

London. In England a special penchant developed for overdoor or mantle panels, whether of single pieces of paper or two sheets joined, often with an engraved outline.

Many of these western designs were similar in subject matter to the Chinese papers from which they derived their inspiration, though they were often very different in feeling. In Brighton Pavilion, however, there was an unusual example of a more abstract interpretation. The King's Bedroom and Library are decorated with an exact replica, painted directly on to the wall, of the green and white wallpaper originally designed by Robert Jones, who worked for Frederick Crace between 1817 and 1823.

52
A painted restoration of the original paper designed by Robert Jones between 1817–1823 and produced by Frederick Crace. From the King's Apartments, Brighton Pavilion.
        Brighton Corporation.

Some unused lengths of this paper, in yellow and grey, survive at the Cooper Hewitt Museum, New York. When restoration was carried out in 1951, after the walls had been covered for a century with distemper and the woodwork heavily varnished, the spare sample sheets of yellow, which the Prince rejected, supplied the pattern, and the original green wallpaper he chose instead, fragments of which were found behind columns in the library, supplied the exact colour. Some unused sheets of the original Chinese trellis-patterned dado were also available, for they had been stored in the Pavilion for many years, and these were placed in the positions for which they had originally been intended.

Crace, Jones's employer, belonged to a family that had already made a considerable contribution to the history of wallpaper. In 1750, Edward Crace had founded a decorating establishment in London and in 1780 he was joined by his son John. Among his patrons were George III and the Prince of Wales. He decorated Drury Lane Theatre, Covent Garden Opera House and Carlton House. John's son Frederick was later employed not only on the Brighton Pavilion project but also on Windsor Castle. Frederick in turn had a son, J. G. Crace (wallpaper's first historian), who became engaged in work for the new Houses of Parliament and did much to encourage better designs and improved standards of production for the wallpaper industry. The Crace firm, which was often concerned with mural painting rather than just wallpaper, was eventually taken over by Cowtan's.

The next major European development was a fashion for high-class wallpaper decorated with silver, gold and bronze. The actual material may have been an amalgam of tin and copper. It was first produced in Holland (the metal used was often called Dutch Metal or Mosaic Gold) and later it spread further south. A Frenchman called De Couvier introduced the process into Bavaria in 1781. Precipitated by the exoticism of chinoiserie, a special taste for silver and gold paper borders emerged, and the same liking for rich shiny metals also became evident in painted decorations. The trend may have combined with another influence that was especially strong at the time, namely the fashion for embossed leather hangings, the skilful production of which had reached a glorious peak. Leather hangings had for a long time employed metal foils, and it is interesting that the new use of silver and gold should start in Holland, where the late blossoming of leather work was most pronounced. The reflective metallicized surfaces had often been used with white in an attempt to catch what light there was in the dimly lit houses which for a long time were the norm. The same delightful combination was used in the wallpapers of this period. The paper itself was tougher and thicker than present-day paper and less prone to discoloration. As it was also darker, a ground of whiting was applied before the addition of the metal.

The quality that was often sought was iridescence, and Robert Dossie in his *Handmaid of the Arts* of 1758 describes the use of 'smalt' (glass

On following pages
Colour 7 *Left*
Wallpaper in the Chinese Drawing Room, Temple Newsam House, Leeds.

Leeds City Council.

Colour 8 *Centre*
Chinese handpainted wallpaper, *c.* 1803, on a white mica ground, inscribed on the back, 'From Merchant Taylor's (who bought it from Sotheby's) Approx date 1803'.

Whitworth Art Gallery, University of Manchester.

Colour 9 *Right*
English handpainted wallpaper, *c.* 1790, attributed to the Eckhardts.

Victoria and Albert Museum, London.

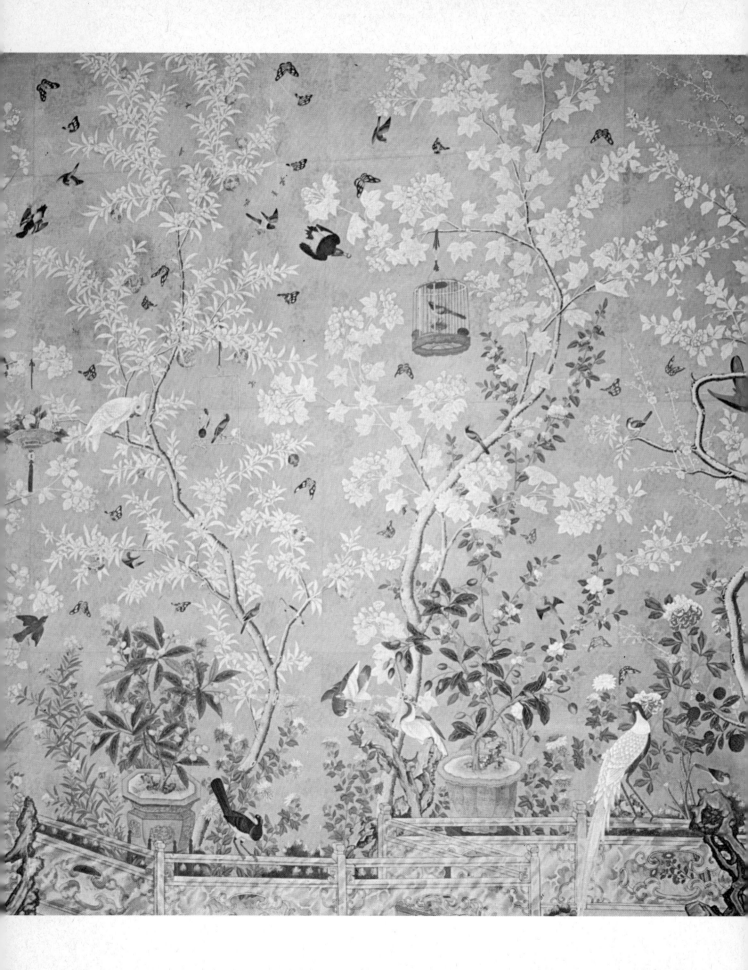

53
'Mother of Pearl' wallpaper by
Herting of Einbeck, Germany,
1850–60.
Deutsches Tapetenmuseum, Kassel.

coloured with zaffre, the impure oxide of cobalt) to give a bright, warm,
blue shining surface. A particularly good sort of smalt was made in Saxony.
Another common way of achieving glitter was by use of the minerals talc
and mica, both of them lustrous silicates, which were powdered and glued
to the paper to give it a silky and pearly sheen, sometimes tinged with a
slight colour which varied according to the mineral's chemical structure.

The vogue for shiny walls had a long life and extended over a wide area.
It was popular, for instance, in Germany, where from 1840 to 1860
Perlmutttapeten (literally, 'mother-of-pearl wallpapers') were produced
by Carl Herting of Einbeck. The floral motifs used in his work all display

an excellent draughtsmanship, and he is known to have kept a sketch book of nature studies as a youth. Gold or silver leaf was applied to the prepared paper which had either been covered with a coloured ground or printed with a pattern, and the surface was then glazed over with thin oil paint, which tinted the wallpaper without obscuring the shimmering design underneath. Herting's wallpapers were exported all over the world. Another notable manufacturer who produced gilded papers, this time in Holland, was called Eccard, and it is tempting to link him with the Eckhardt brothers who had started making wallpaper in London in the 1770s. Some of their work too was ornamented with silver and gold. The exact date when they set up business is not known. Although Lyson, in his *Environs of London,* claims that their factory opened in 1786, Anthony George Eckhardt took out a patent for printing silks and cottons, muslins and calicoes and papers in 1774, shortly before he was made a Fellow of the Royal Society. In 1791, the brothers moved to a new factory near the King's Road and Sloane Street, where they are said to have employed over four hundred girls to execute the considerable amount of hand-painting that was used in combination with engraving from copper plates. There is little work that can be attributed to them with certainty, although they maintained that every article produced by them was stamped with their mark. They must have been very inventive, since they took out many patents. A contemporary leaflet describes their work as including stucco effects and papers which could be taken down, cleaned and replaced. The high standard of their work, moreover, was extolled by both their

54
English wallpaper, *c.*1790, possibly by the Eckhardt Brothers. Block printed in polychrome distemper. From George Hill House, Sussex.
Whitworth Art Gallery, University of Manchester.

contemporaries and successors. J. G. Crace described them as 'gentlemen of considerable taste and spirit whose paper hangings were of such elegance and beauty as far surpassed those of all other countries'.

In London at the time, there was another wallpaper manufacturer of great repute, although again no work which can be certainly identified as his has yet been discovered. His name was John Sherringham, and he became famous for his 'arabesque' papers in the French style, which he probably first took to manufacturing after his travels round Europe. Although his business lasted only sixteen years, his reputation was such that Mawer Cowtan, many years later, referred to him as the 'Wedgwood of the Paperstainers'. One of his artists was 'Fusili', and it is interesting to conjecture whether this might have been the painter Johann Heinrich Füssli from Zurich, who later changed his name to Henry Fuseli. Starting in business slightly later than the Eckhardts, Sherringham too had a reputation for fine detail and pleasant subtle colours.

In 1773, the laws on the importation of foreign papers into England were relaxed, and this brought to the attention of English customers the high quality of French design.

Although the work of many of the French manufacturers survives, one man overshadows the rest: Jean-Baptiste Réveillon. Apprenticed to a haberdasher and stationer in 1741, he worked for other people until 1752, when he purchased the lease for premises of his own, where he sold, among other things, imported English wallpapers. In Paris many designers imitated the English style, especially when trading difficulties between the two countries during the Seven Years War had made the originals harder to come by. Réveillon soon came to excel at producing his own papers, and in 1763 he bought a site at the Folie Titon, the main building of which he was later to acquire also.

Réveillon was something of a showman, but he was also thoughtful, skilled and hardworking. He worked in flock and also adopted the use of distemper colours, as the English were doing, and brought a new quality to their production. He used original designs from excellent designers, some of whom were involved in the Gobelins' tapestry factory and were therefore much influenced by designs for woven materials. Herculaneum had been discovered during the mid-eighteenth century, and designs influenced by this enjoyed a vogue for a time, along with imitations of architectural ornaments, deeply imbued with classical feeling.

Although it cannot be said that Réveillon was a great innovator, he was a great organizer and a remarkable perfectionist. One of his overriding priorities was to have paper of a suitable quality for his products, and he made full use of the invention of insoluble colours, attributed by Phyllis Ackerman to the Duc de Chaulnes. Previously, only Chinese papers had perfect insolubility; European colours smudged if the papers were not hung extremely carefully. But the new invention prevented this sort of disaster.

Colour 10 *Opposite left*
Decorative panel, *c.* 1785–88, from a design by Jean-Baptiste Fay. Block printed by Réveillon with distemper on a coloured ground.
    Musée des Arts Décoratifs, Paris.

Colour 11 *Opposite right*
A typical French wallpaper of *c.* 1800.
    Deutsches Tapetenmuseum, Kassel.

81

Réveillon aimed to serve three different markets. He produced luxury
papers with beautiful and elaborate designs costing as much as tapestries;
papers known as 'communs', which used seven or eight blocks and catered
for the bourgeoisie; and very simple papers which used only one colour. In
1785 he was awarded the Necker medal for the Encouragement of the
Useful Arts.

82

56
Two panels by Réveillon, *c.* 1789, one representing the fruits of the autumn. Both are block printed with distemper on a coloured ground.
Musée des Arts Décoratifs, Paris.

What next went amiss is somewhat confused. Whether Réveillon
became an innocent victim, or whether he had indeed exploited his
workmen and refused to listen to their protests, is not known. But
whatever the cause, on the very brink of the French Revolution his factory
was stormed, ruined and most of his property burnt. Réveillon fled to
England, later sending evidence back to prove that he had not underpaid
his men; but to no avail. After about two years, his firm was taken over by
Jacquemart and Bénard, who somewhat tactfully specialized in papers
bearing Republican motifs—caps of liberty, tri-coloured paper ribbons
and the rest. Indeed, they were commissioned in 1792 to produce
revolutionary papers for all the national palaces and administrative
buildings. Many of these, however, were not actually delivered, for the
finances of the new regime were unreliable, and the vogue for political
interior decorating soon passed. One of the surprising aspects of the
Revolution is that despite its tragic consequences for individual producers
in the wallpaper industry (as in other trades), it had little profound effect
on output or on standards of manufacture generally. France swept on to a
peak of very original quality in wallpaper. Production soared and varieties
multiplied, and much of this can be attributed to the example of Réveillon,
of whom the French wallpaper historian Henri Clouzot once said: 'He
gave wallpaper a new language to speak.'

Another casualty of the French Revolution was the firm of Arthur and
Robert, who produced complete room schemes of extraordinary quality,
particularly in sepia and grisaille. Arthur's fate was to become involved in
politics, and he was executed in 1794 as an accomplice of Robespierre. His
predecessor in the firm, René Grenard, was also condemned to death a few
days later, so Robert carried on the firm alone, prefixing his name with the
appellation 'Citoyen'.

America strongly felt the leadership of Europe in wallpaper design in the
eighteenth century as many present-day American papers will indicate, for
they are careful reproductions of imports of the period to be found

UNITE·INDIVISIBILITE
DE·LA·RÉPUBLIQUE
LIBERTE·EGALITE
FRATERNITÉ·OULA·MORT

59
Design for a wallpaper by Jacquemart
et Bénard, 1798.
    Musée des Arts Décoratifs, Paris.

throughout the country's museums. The tendency was to buy from abroad
rather than home-produce, and so there was not much scope for new
designs to be tested. There were practical reasons for this. The most

60
Stencilling on wood sheathing,
c. 1830, in a bedroom at Joshua Lasalle
House, Connecticut, USA.
American Museum in Britain, Bath.

significant one was that in America, until the beginning of the nineteenth
century, there was a scarcity of rags, and the use of wood pulp in paper
manufacture had not yet been developed. Yet the extent to which
wallpaper was used in American homes should not be underestimated. In
advertisements, large selections were offered, and it seems likely that such
availability would indicate considerable demand. It is probable that
American manufacturers imported stocks of paper hangings to decorate
themselves. Wallpaper manufacturers have rarely been involved directly
with the production of their paper themselves, so such a practice would not
be far outside the normal method of trading. It is interesting to note that
the purchase of American-made paper hangings was urged as a patriotic
gesture, although one vendor of imported papers criticized the colours of
home-produced work as being too pale and fugitive.

The custom of wall-stencilling, already mentioned as one of the ancestors of wallpaper, also flourished in America during this period, partly because of the difficulties listed above. It was usual to have a scene, probably a landscape, for the overmantel, particularly in the parlour, and although sometimes done on canvas and set in the woodwork, this was very often painted direct on the plaster, which had often been given a coloured wash beforehand. Fire boards were often painted with a vase of flowers. The walls themselves were commonly painted with the devices of wallpaper, such as borders, friezes and pilaster designs, and many of the currently popular wallpaper motifs. Eventually scenic murals became popular, probably under the influence of the French scenic wallpapers which were to be so widely admired and bought during the nineteenth century. A particularly interesting example is a paper commemorating the death of Washington. Legend has it that a room's worth of this paper was presented to the governor of each state.

Many of the extant wallpapers of this period in America are to be found covering hatboxes and bandboxes (see Colour Plate 12). Covering papers especially designed for hatboxes usually gave some indication of the contents, but these seem to be in the minority. The common practice was to use spare pieces of wallpaper. Engravings were used occasionally too, but these must have been relatively hard to come by. Although many of these papers are of a later period than that covered by this chapter, their feeling of quiet, unostentatious skill and the delicacy of the patterns chosen place them stylistically in the Age of Gentility. Their subject matter makes an interesting commentary on American life in the early nineteenth century. Several depict Napoleon, a character for whom America seemed to feel considerable sympathy, while others show the curious animals which were paraded in travelling exhibitions (precursors of today's circuses). There was a special fashion for wallpaper showing birds, particularly parrots, and this reflects the passing interest in pet caged birds, which is especially evident in the wallpaper covering the hatboxes. The bald eagle, chosen as a device to represent the country, and commonly a symbol of liberty, also figures in wallpapers. Bird motifs were popular in England too, not only in wallpaper but also in textiles and ceramics. Pine cones, pineapples (symbols of hospitality) and pomegranates, rather like the ones so frequently found in medieval textiles, and in the Cambridge Fragments, were equally fashionable among the motifs for these late eighteenth and early nineteenth century American papers. The pillar, used extensively in textiles at this time, is well represented, but is far outnumbered by examples of the drapery swag, which was common everywhere.

The early nineteenth century preoccupation with transport is reflected in the sailing ships, steamboats, and coaching scenes which seem to have adorned the walls of many American homes. Other wallpapers refer to political events. The bandbox second from the top on the right in our

61
Wallpaper commemorating George
Washington, produced by Ebenezer
Clough in Boston, 1800. Block
printed in black white and grey on a
blue ground.
Cooper Hewitt Museum of
Decorative Arts and Design,
Smithsonian Institution, New York.

SACRED
TO
WASHINGTON

62
A frieze incorporating the drapery
swag, a common motif at the end of
the eighteenth century. Printed by the
Remondini family in Italy.
Museo Civico di Bassano
del Grappa.

63
An example from Denmark of the
drapery swag motif.
Nationalmuseet, Copenhagen.

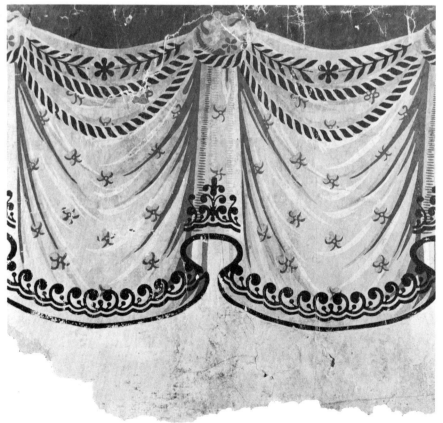

illustration (Colour Plate 12) depicts the successful candidate in the presidential elections of 1840—William Henry Harrison, who died one month after taking office. Another president, Andrew Jackson, also known as 'Old Hickory', can be seen on the seventh bandbox from the top in the third row from the left.

In Europe and America, it was the literary, documentary and celebratory elements in interior decoration which largely dominated the beginning of the nineteenth century. This is already evident in the French Revolutionary papers, and in many of the wallpapers used on the hatboxes and bandboxes, but it was from the early 1800s onwards, when the industrial societies began to be proud of their accumulating achievements and eager to pay themselves tribute, that the pictorial, celebratory trend really began to gather speed.

Magnificence and Mediocrity

TRADE had expanded prodigiously during the 1800s, and as the nineteenth century dawned in the newly industrialized countries, many people, seeing the way things were going flocked to the towns to augment and hopefully to share the growing prosperity of the manufacturers. For the first generation of industrialists, at every level from workmen to managers and owners, home decoration became a project on which more money and thought could be lavished than ever before. Wallpaper seemed more to their taste than any other type of mural decoration and satisfied their needs better, and before long it became a growth industry. The results of this expanding market were twofold. On the one hand, the guaranteed outlet meant that enormously ambitious papers could be produced, hand-printed with a care, skill, patience and financial commitment that seem incredible to us today. Yet at the same time, undermining this tendency, frantic attempts to supply a growing need led to standards of design becoming secondary to quantity of output. Which of these tendencies was dominant depended on how rapidly the Industrial Revolution was taking place in the particular area under scrutiny. The first approach was found mainly in France, where the less dramatic impact of industrialization and its rather late development meant that to some degree the Age of Gentility was prolonged. There is, however, a slight air of vulgarity and showmanship even about French wallpapers of this time which firmly links them with their contemporaries in Europe and America. This is not to cast aspersions on their achievements, though, which manufacturers in other countries greatly admired and envied.

The most striking examples of the new French manner were the 'scenics', the term used to describe *trompe l'œil* landscapes on a grand scale, not repeating but creating a complete scene around the walls of a room, seeming to melt them away in an illusion of infinite space. There was a proven interest in viewing landscapes of this sort even before these wallpapers were produced. E. A. Entwisle in his book *French Scenic Wallpapers* points out that there were dioramas in London at the beginning of the nineteenth century, and they had existed in France even earlier. They took the form of landscapes arranged on the inside of a cylindrical surface or rolled out as a continuous passing scene before the spectator, like an early version of the cinema. The scenic wallpapers not only fulfilled a decorative function but also an educational one. Mothers taught daughters (boys, of course, were more likely to be at school) using wallpaper as a visual aid. Geography, history, literature—every possible subject was covered in one or other of the scenics.

The best known producer of scenic wallpapers was Jean Zuber, a draper's son born in Mulhouse on 1 May 1773. He joined a printed textiles firm as a commercial traveller responsible for orders not only from his own country but also from Italy, Switzerland and Spain. However, in 1797 the free city of Mulhouse was surrounded with a commercial blockade by the French customs, and in order to escape it the firm for which Zuber worked acquired the Commandery of the Teutonic Order at Rixheim, which had become national property after the French Revolution. Zuber was entrusted with the moving of the whole factory. At the new site, the company prospered, for as well as its excellent wallpaper produced from paper made at its own mill, it also manufactured dyes and various chemicals.

In 1802, Zuber became the sole proprietor and adopted a policy, often followed in France, of employing first-class designers. His organizational powers must have been exceptional, for the planning involved in the production of scenic papers was elaborate and painstaking. Quite long periods would elapse between each new design. Once the blocks were made, the designs were reproduced for many years, and some were still being used in the twentieth century. It was absolutely essential to sell each design over a considerable number of years in order to recoup the enormous outlay. Up to two thousand blocks had to be cut, so each new project was a great financial gamble, expensive in terms of not only the material necessary for blocks of extra strength to be made, but also the time spent on the job by the engraver, and by the artist, who closely supervised the work throughout. In some cases, blocks were slightly altered to meet new situations. Figures were added or removed, for instance, to match changed political circumstances. One paper, first sold from 1834 to 1836 as 'Views of North America', (Plate 74), was reissued in 1838 as 'The American War of Independence', merely with the addition of a few figures. Zuber produced many geographical panoramas of this type, the first of which was 'Views of Switzerland', issued in about 1803. He strove tirelessly to improve the quality of his products, visiting England to inspect the mechanical advances there and afterwards implementing changes in his factory in a measured and thoughtful way.

The major rival to Zuber's firm was Dufour and Leroy. Dufour, at the age of fifty-six, opened a factory in Paris in 1808, where he employed two to three hundred people. One of his early successes was 'The Savages of the Pacific Ocean' of 1806, otherwise known as 'The Voyages of Captain Cook', which was designed by Charvet and was issued with a booklet as a

64
Wallpaper panel designed by Joseph Laurent Malaine (1745–1809), produced by Jean Zuber.
Musée des Arts Décoratifs, Paris.

93

65
Chinoiserie style wallpaper produced
by Zuber about 1860, one of a group
designed by Poterlet and Guichard.
    Musée des Arts Décoratifs, Paris.

commentary to the scenes. Produced at about the same time was 'The
Months of the Year', designed by Fragonard *fils,* and another of his notable
designers, who came later, was Xavier Mader. He worked for Dufour for
fifteen years, and one of the wallpapers he produced during this time was
'The Monuments of Paris'. The fame of Dufour, however, rests very
largely on his set of scenic wallpapers based on the legends of Cupid and
Psyche. It was designed by Lafitte, possibly helped by Blondell, but it is
Mader who is said to have supervised the cutting of the blocks. The designs
were shorter than usual, being only five feet seven inches high. Normally

67
'The Incas', one panel of a scenic
wallpaper produced by Dufour et
Compagnie 1826 and based on the
book by Marmontel on the conquest
of Peru by Pizarro (1531) *The Incas or
the destruction of the empire of Peru*.
  Musée des Arts Décoratifs, Paris.

66
'August', one of a series of twelve
panels representing the months,
attributed to Alexandre-Evariste
Fragonard (1780–1850). First
produced by Dufour et Compagnie, *c.*
1808.
  Whitworth Art Gallery,
  University of Manchester.

95

they were between eight and ten feet high with plenty of allowance for adjustment (for example lots of blank sky which could be removed without spoiling the picture) and space for the addition of borders, dados or other ornaments at the bottom. The number of lengths in one set varied from five to thirty or more, and each roll was numbered, and sometimes named, to ensure that the right sequence appeared on the walls.

Dufour's daughter married Amable Leroy, who had been a commander in the Garde Nationale. He joined his father-in-law's firm and was responsible for, among other projects, a scenic wallpaper by the name of 'The Campaigns of the French Armies in Italy' printed in grisaille. Meanwhile, Dufour was also producing wallpapers which had every appearance of satin curtains, embroidered and trimmed with lace, folded and pleated in every way, and hung with tassels and decorative ornaments. There was a vogue at this time for actual woven material treated in this way, and many of Dufour's wallpapers are remarkable for the skill and elegance with which they imitated this fashion.

In 1836 the business was taken over by Dufour's manager Lapeyre and his partner Drouard, who produced a few modest scenics, but in 1865 the company was purchased by Desfossé and Karth. Under new ownership

68
Two panels from the series illustrating the story of Cupid and Psyche, first produced by Dufour in 1816. Block printed in distemper grisaille.
Whitworth Art Gallery,
University of Manchester.

69
'The Monuments of Paris', a scenic wallpaper produced by Dufour.
Victoria and Albert Museum,
London.

70 *Opposite*
Three *trompe l'œil* papers by Dufour et Compagnie, Paris.
(a) 'Satin Curtain', 1810–12.
(b) 'White Satin Curtain', 1810.
(c) 'White Satin Curtain', *c*.1812.
Musée des Arts Décoratifs, Paris.

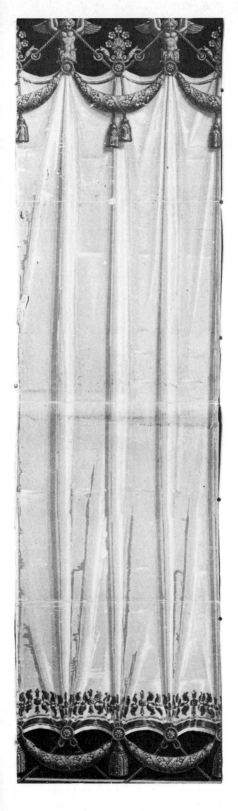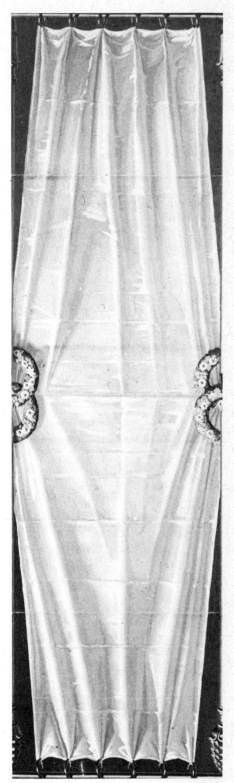

97

99

Anonymous French wallpaper,
1850–60, imitating a lace curtain.
Musée des Arts Décoratifs, Paris.

On previous pages
Colour 12 *Left*
Hatboxes and bandboxes covered in
American wallpapers from the first
half of the nineteenth century.
Shelburne Museum, Vermont.

Colour 13 *Right*
Panel from 'Décor Chinois', a set of
ten panels first produced by Jean
Zuber in 1832. Production continued
well into this century and it is unlikely
that this example is from a nineteenth
century edition. Block printed in
polychrome distemper on a white
mica ground.
Whitworth Art Gallery,
University of Manchester.

the firm produced some very beautiful scenics, not so much in the grand
historical mode as in a quieter and more intimate character. Two of the
designers, Muller and Dumont, were remarkable flower painters, and their
work for this firm, in some ways very typical of the Second Empire period
in France, was also perhaps the most successful.

Another contemporary French manufacturer was Jean-Baptiste Daup-
tain, whose son and daughter continued to run the firm after his death.
They produced innumerable papers in later years in a rather crisp
architectural style with a touch of Gothic.

Mader, designer for Dufour, also ran his own wallpaper firm with his
son, and when he died in 1830 it was carried on by his widow and managed

by Etienne Delicourt (who was active in the wallpaper industry from about 1838 to 1860) until the sons were old enough to take over themselves. When this happened, Delicourt set up business on his own, and won the first prize at London's Great Exhibition of 1851 for an impressive paper entitled 'The Great Hunt', for which four thousand blocks were used.

One index of the success of the French scenic wallpapers was that they were extensively exported. Numerous examples are to be found in American houses. One of them, Zuber's 'Views of North America' in its early pre-military version (based on engravings of the 1820s and showing five outstanding tourist attractions: Niagara, the Natural Bridge of Virginia, Boston Harbour, West Point and New York Bay) is now in the Diplomatic Reception Room at the White House. It was put there in 1961, after being removed in small pieces from an old house in Maryland and reassembled like a jigsaw puzzle. Although wallpapers were used extensively in the White House immediately after its construction, none of the ones hung then were scenic. The oval-shaped room into which this particular one was transferred, however, is particularly suited to such a paper, for here the illusion of its panorama is unspoilt by corners. In lesser buildings too, scenic papers were extraordinarily popular, not only in America, but also in Ireland, for example, where at Clonskeagh Castle, Milltown, County Dublin, there still hangs a full set of Dufour's 'Bay of Naples', one of his cheaper papers which was brought out in shades of green, sepia, mauve or bistre as well as the more common grisaille. But in England French scenics did not catch on, and the English, either on account of the tax on imports or a feeling of patriotic pride, continued to prefer their own products.

At this time English creativity in the field of wallpaper production was channelled into perfecting the mechanics rather than pushing back artistic boundaries. In 1739 Louis Robert, a Frenchman, had made a prototype of a machine which successfully produced long lengths of paper. His experiments occupied his spare time over a period of several years. After much delay and crossing of the Channel, the Foudrinier brothers, Henry and Sealy, well-known stationers, purchased a one third share in the patents. The machine was perfected by Bryan Donkin, a clever mechanic working for John Hall, millwright of Dartford. Using a continuous belt of moving wire screen to produce the paper, it was the most successful of the early paper-making machines and those in use today remain very similar. The excise authorities in England would not allow the use of continuous paper until 1830, however, and so like many important inventions, the machine brought little money to those originally responsible for its development, even though it did open the way for the industrialization of the wallpaper business. Zuber started using 'endless paper' about 1820. In 1827 the first Foudrinier machine was imported into America. There were other paper-making machines being introduced at this time, notably one developed by John Dickinson which used a cylinder to form the paper, but

72
A panel depicting a hunting trophy in grisaille, French, probably by Delicourt.

Whitworth Art Gallery,
University of Manchester.

On following pages
Colour 14 *Left*
Part of a Tiger Hunting scene produced by Dufour et Compagnie, 1815. The full series comprised twenty-five panels.

Whitworth Art Gallery,
University of Manchester.

Colour 15 *Right*
'White Satin Curtain', produced by Dufour et Compagnie, Paris 1820–5.

Musée des Arts Décoratifs, Paris.

101

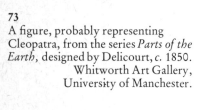

73
A figure, probably representing
Cleopatra, from the series *Parts of the
Earth*, designed by Delicourt, *c.* 1850.
Whitworth Art Gallery,
University of Manchester.

74 *Left and opposite right*
'Views of North America', produced
by Zuber, 1834–6.
(a) 'Boston Harbour'
(b) 'Niagara Falls'
(c) 'Marching Grounds, United
    States Military Academy'
        The White House Collection,
            Washington D.C.

75
'Bacchus and Bacchante', produced
by the Fabrique Lyonnaise at the
beginning of the nineteenth century,
giving the effect of patinated bronze
figures against a blue ground.
        Musée des Arts Décoratifs, Paris.

106

none seems to have been as successful as the Foudriniers'. In spite of these new ventures, handmade paper continued to be made and used for wallpaper manufacture until well into the 1870s.

Paper at this time was much more like woven material than it had been previously, and it was inevitable therefore that those involved in the mechanization of wallpaper production should experiment with the techniques of fabric printing. However, the thick distemper colours used for wallpapers would not print well from the engraved copper cylinders of the machines, and neither would the paper receive the image as readily as, say, calico, so there was plenty of room for improvement. During the 1830s experiments were made to adapt textile roller printing machines so that they could be used for wallpaper. Credit for the final breakthrough belongs to the Potters of Darwen where one of the employees, Walmsley Preston, converted a calico printing machine by using surface rollers with a raised pattern, as in block printing. Potters' machine-printed papers came on to the market in 1841. By that time the firm had combined their 'surface rollers' with an efficient system for feeding colour to them. The rollers were made of a wooden core with the outlines of the designs formed by strips of brass tapped into the wood and filled in where necessary with felt to the same level as the strips. The machine itself was very similar to those used today, though the rollers are now sometimes marked photographically, and rubber and other materials have recently been tried as replacements for the wood and brass. The blank paper is drawn from a large reel suspended high on one side of the machine. The paper then revolves around the central drum which is surrounded by printing rollers, each with its own trough of colour and a feeding belt which coats it in ink. When printed the paper is drawn by rollers along to the drying chambers full of steam boxes.

Printing did lose some of its flexibility through industrialization. Designs had to be of an exact size and could not be turned as with hand blocks. Also it was not advisable to have both large masses and fine lines on the same rollers or uneven printing would result. However, some of the cheaper wallpapers (of, say, two colours on thin paper) could be produced at a rate of 420 pieces (rolls) an hour, as opposed to the 300 rolls per day that a good workman could print by hand. It seems likely that such machines were imported into America to the Howell factory in 1844, although simpler, American-made machines may have been in use before this. The first American printing machine is sometimes credited to Josiah Bumstead in 1835, but the descriptions of this and other machines of the period, including the one imported by John Howell, are too vague to give a clear picture of the exact state of mechanization that had been achieved in America at this time.

Simultaneously a revolution was taking place in domestic lighting. During the eighteenth century lighting had depended largely on candles, but with the turn of the century both gas and Colza oil lamps came into

PRINTING THE PAPER

76
Printing the Paper as illustrated in a drawing of Christy, Shepherd and Garett, New York. From *Scientific American* July 24, 1880. Photo by courtesy of the Science and Technology Research Centre, New York Public Library. Astor Lennox and Tilden Foundations.

use, to be followed by the rather explosive but much brighter lamphine lamps between 1830 and 1850. In 1859 mineral oil was discovered as a practicable fuel, and soon afterwards the petroleum lamp was providing millions of homes with safe and bright illumination. It may have been due partly to the decreasing need for light-reflective walls and partly to popular interest in the newly discovered murals of Herculaneum that darker colours came into favour in the wallpapers of the time, particularly the dark reds and greens often associated with the Victorian era in England. There was also perhaps the practical consideration that darker walls would tolerate more kindly the rapidly worsening pollution given off by the growing industries. It is possible too that these colours were often chosen out of a concern for propriety. Sober luxury rather than brash self-advertisement was thought fitting for the leaders of a prosperous empire.

Because of mechanical developments and the advantageous trading agreements possible for powerful western countries, the price of wallpaper fell throughout the century, making it an enormously popular commodity. But it must not be imagined that the wallpaper machines were welcomed immediately and wholeheartedly, or that they were totally without their evils. A machine introduced at Clarkes of High Holborn, London, produced a strike among the workmen, and the Government had to send in troops to protect the establishment. In 1832 a government report

in England pointed out that the use of arsenic and white lead in the colouring materials at wallpaper factories was causing sickness, loss of appetite and headaches among the workers, and possibly respiratory troubles as well. Arsenic was later banned from the pigments and, many firms advertised their products as non-arsenical. Arsenic and copper combinations had before this been used extensively, especially for the popular green wallpapers, but these were now considered dangerous even to the occupants of rooms where they were hung, for minute particles would detach themselves easily from the paper and diffuse through the air.

In 1862 another British Government enquiry into child labour in the paperstaining business pointed out the prevalence of drunkenness among paperstainers. This may have been caused by the heat of the 'hot shops' (or drying chambers), where the newly printed papers were hung. The use of mica, talc and similar materials, and the process of flocking must also have caused considerable dust. The powdered earth colours customarily used and the China clay or Paris white with which they were mixed must have been an additional hazard to the lungs. The children who laboured in the factories are said to have been healthy, but when they worked overtime for hours on end the foremen, we learn from contemporary evidence, had to 'bawl at them to keep them awake'.*

Demand for wallcoverings kept pace with increased production. When wallpaper seemed too much of a luxury, houseowners resorted to less sophisticated methods. Later in the century, a description of a privy in Flora Thompson's *Lark Rise to Candleford* hints not only at a fastidious concern to decorate wall-space but also at the high level of political awareness, often chauvinistic, that was making inroads even into more orthodox schemes.

> On the wall of the 'little house' at Laura's home pictures cut from the newspapers were pasted. These were changed when the walls were whitewashed and in succession they were 'The Bombardment of Alexandria', all clouds of smoke, flying fragments and flashes of explosives; 'Glasgow's Mournful Disaster: Plunges from Life from the Daphne' with the end of the train dangling from the broken bridge over a boiling sea. It was before the days of Press photography and the artists were able to give their imagination full play. Later, the place of honour in the 'little house' was occupied by 'Our Political Leaders', two rows of portraits on one print: Mr Gladstone, with hawk-like countenance and flashing eyes, in the middle of the top row, and kind, sleepy-looking Lord Salisbury in the other. Laura loved that picture because Lord Randolph Churchill was there. She thought he must be the most handsome man in the world.

The particular interests itemized in this extract—battles, political figures and current events—had a particular appeal for the Victorian English, and a spate of commemorative wallpapers on these themes was produced. Another common subject for designs was the Queen, particularly her Coronation and Jubilee, and this was a feature in interior decoration which has survived until very recently, the latest symptoms of the craze, now dying, being the photographs of Queen Elizabeth on display in both private homes and public buildings. There were numerous literary wallpapers too, showing characters and scenes from books and plays.

Many of the later examples of these designs were printed by the 'Sanitary Process', which entailed the use not of the raised rollers which had finally been adopted for normal printing, but of intaglio-engraved copper cylinders, like those used for calico printing, which had been unsuccess-

* See E. A. Entwisle *Wallpapers of the Victorian Era* F. Lewis, Leigh-on-Sea, 1964

78
Commemorative wallpaper showing
the battles of the Duke of Wellington,
probably produced by Heywood,
Higginbottom & Smith, and therefore
c. 1853–5.
Victoria and Albert Museum,
London.

79
Diamond Jubilee Commemorative
Frieze, 1897. 'Sanitary' machine
printed in six colours.
Whitworth Art Gallery,
University of Manchester.

80
English paper decoration showing
Edward VII and Queen Alexandra,
c. 1901. Colour lithograph.
Whitworth Art Gallery,
University of Manchester.

81
'Fête Galante', scenic border,
English, late nineteenth century.
'Sanitary' machine print.
Whitworth Art Gallery,
University of Manchester.

fully tried for ordinary wallpaper printing almost half a century before. Shortly after their introduction in 1884, multicoloured wallpapers produced by this method became the fad of the moment, rather like vinyl papers at the beginning of the 1960s. Although the Sanitary papers could be either matt or glossy, the colours used (in a base of turpentine and resin) were more subdued than those used for surface printing, and there is a certain blandness about their texture.

Sanitary papers proved to be merely an ephemeral fashion, as did so

115

82
Two paper ceiling rosettes.
(a) English, second half nineteenth
    century.
        Victoria and Albert Museum,
                            London.
(b) German, 1860–70.
    Deutsches Tapetenmuseum, Kassel.

many of the ideas in wallpaper at this time. There was a great inventiveness in the air, but many of the results were slight and superficial. Much effort was put into producing imitative designs. Clever representations of plaster-work abounded, some in the form of ceiling roses which could be changed more frequently than the rest of the décor, since the gas or oil lighting darkened them more quickly. There was much in the way of imitation wood, marbling and *trompe l'œil* statue effects. Dufour was an expert at the latter and his standards were far above the general level in England.

By far the greatest number of wallpapers produced in Britain were over-ornate *trompe l'œil* floral designs produced by manufacturers because that was what the public wanted, and bought by the public because that was what was available—a vicious circle which to some extent still prevails today. Nevertheless, to the earnest and commercially-minded Victorians, the vulgarity of public taste and the poor standard of British products were far more a matter of concern and education than they are now. In 1832 Sir Robert Peel supported a motion in the House of Commons that the National Gallery should be established to help refine the taste of both the public and the manufacturers. Unfortunately, the failure of many designers to cope with the very rapid changes within the wallpaper industry, and the unreal and antiquated aspects of what meagre art education there was at this time were problems not so easily to be put right. A common reaction of designers who were encouraged to visit art galleries was simply to copy the paintings they saw there. There was a fashion, in fact, for 'fine art' pictorial wallpapers, though the reproductions that appeared on them were generally inferior in quality to similar work that was being produced in France at the time. They were sometimes of medieval and romantic subjects and must have appealed to much the same appetite as that which was satisfied also by papers in imitation of Gothic architecture.

In pursuit of an improvement in taste, the Normal School of Design was set up by the Board of Trade, and in 1846 eleven provincial Branch Schools were given government support. In the following year Henry Cole formed his firm of Summerly's Art Manufactures. His propagandist abilities in the cause of art education proved greater than his abilities as a designer, but he did inspire the admiration and friendship of Prince Albert, and together they planned the Great Exhibition of 1851.

Whatever the merits of the exhibits themselves, the Great Exhibition attracted vast numbers of visitors and aroused an enormous interest in qualities of design. The wallpaper submitted covered twenty-five thousand square feet of wall-space. Yet the British wallpaper industry did not emerge from the venture in a very good light. The first prize was won by the Frenchman Delicourt. The efforts of the British manufacturers were condemned as over-ornate, and the jurors attacked them for failing to observe the basic rules of design.

83
Copy of Murillo's painting *Boys with Bread* produced by Jeffrey & Co., London, *c.* 1843.
Victoria and Albert Museum, London.

Among the exhibitors were the firms of Townsend, Horne and Jeffrey, who showed a frieze depicting a portion of the Elgin Marbles; William Woollams, a pupil of Sherringham, who showed a pilaster design, using between sixty and seventy blocks; Crace; W. B. Simpson; Turner and Williams, who displayed a 'glancing' design, that is to say one whose lights and darks change as the viewer progresses across the room; and Scott Cuthbertson, who had a Tudor-style gold and white paper. Despite their

84
Anonymous French Gothic
wallpaper, 1835–45.
      Musée des Arts Décoratifs, Paris.

85
Anonymous English Gothic
wallpaper, *c.* 1840–50.
      Victoria and Albert Museum,
      London.

86
'Rebecca and the Templar', produced by Delicourt, one of a series of figurative scenes in grisaille.
Whitworth Art Gallery, University of Manchester.

87
'Scheherezade', German wallpaper illustrating the '1001 Nights'. Printed by William Sattler Schweinfurt, *c.*1850.
Deutsches Tapetenmuseum, Kassel.

efforts, a large number of very hostile books, magazines and pamphlets were produced in reaction to the Exhibition. These were written from very varied viewpoints, but what they had in common was a unanimous antagonism. The *Supplementary Report on Design* by Richard Redgrave, one of the jurors, was the first. Matthew Digby Wyatt's contribution to the issue was *Industrial Arts of the Nineteenth Century* (1851) and Gottfried Semper wrote *Wissenschaft, Industrie und Kunst.* In 1856 there was a French report on design by Comte Laborde. These and many of the books which followed were either imported to America or published there as well in subsequent editions. They had a very great influence there, though they seem not to have provoked any particular original movement.

The money from the 1851 Exhibition (some £186,000) was used to buy the site at South Kensington for various museums and colleges, one of which, of course, was the Victoria and Albert Museum, which was to have such an important effect on the next generation of designers. Henry Cole was in charge of the School of Design set up there and moved the exhibits from his own Museum of Manufactures to the South Kensington site. The Museum may have proved more educational that the school itself, which met with much criticism. Ruskin for instance was in his moralistic way a bitter opponent of Cole, finding him bleak, pompous and commercial, and George Moore dismissed Cole's efforts as being merely superficial.

89
'Elvire', border and sidewall, modern reprint of a French wallpaper of the mid-nineteenth century, exported to America, imitating plaid.
   Brunschwig & Fils Inc., New York.

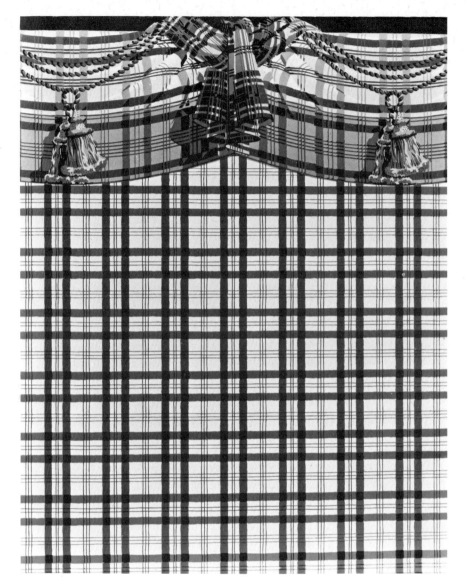

88
Ferronerie baroque, French wallpaper 1840–50.
   Musée des Arts Décoratifs, Paris.

Another result of the exhibition, rather ironically, was a selection of commemorative wallpapers depicting the Crystal Palace. Despite the long-term effects of the enterprise, in the short term the manufacturers themselves continued along the same paths as before. They submitted pieces again to the 1862 Exhibition, only to receive for the most part the same criticisms with the added comment that their colours were muddy. France and Austria, on the other hand, who also exhibited, were highly commended.

John Stewart, writing in the *Art Journal* in 1861, accused the English manufacturers of narrow-mindedness and petty meanness. A reply in the *Manchester Daily Examiner and Times,* probably from the Potters, drew

120

90
English commemorative wallpaper
showing the International Exhibition
at South Kensington, 1862. Machine
printed.
Victoria and Albert Museum,
London.

91
'Supper at the House of Gold',
machine printed by Jules Desfossé,
1862, after a painting by Thomas
Couture.
Victoria and Albert Museum,
London.

attention to the fact that Britain did have some excellent designers and that
the Government, so keen now to raise artistic standards since it found that
exports depended on them, had not given much help in the past. Crippling
taxation was hardly an incentive to take commercial risks and cut down on
what were, for whatever reasons, successful ranges of wallpaper.

There were exhibitions of the same sort in other countries, in 1855 in

92
Two wallpapers incorporating the
German emblem.
(a) Flock, produced by
    Flammersheim, Köln,
    handprinted, *c.* 1858.
(b) Produced by Erismann & Cie,
    1870–71, for a shooting and
    gymnastic festival.
    Deutsches Tapetenmuseum, Kassel.

93
American wallpaper incorporating
'Japanesque' pattern with scenes from
America, 1880–85. Machine printed.
Cooper Hewitt Museum of
Decorative Arts and Design,
Smithsonian Institution, New York.

94
German wallpaper showing sporting
activities, after 1900. Machine
printed.
 Deutsches Tapetenmuseum, Kassel.

95
English wallpaper commemorating
the Boer War 1899–1902. 'Sanitary'
machine printed.
Whitworth Art Gallery,
University of Manchester.

126

Paris for example, and many museums were founded in Europe during the first half of the nineteenth century. From the point of view of wallpaper design and production however, none of this interest was as influential, ultimately, as the controversial bid for self-improvement that took place in London circles of design and commerce between 1840 and 1862.

New Brooms

IN a book that attempts to be international in its scope, I perhaps ought to apologize for devoting a large part of an entire chapter to a short period in England alone. But just as the industrialization of the wallpaper trade was largely initiated in England in the first half of the nineteenth century, so too it was the English who reacted most intensely and creatively to the dangers and limitations of the industrial age. The influence of English designers on Europe reached great heights at the end of the nineteenth century and to a large extent their innovations were the root from which the very different major developments of the future would branch. Before long, however, the cultural lead passed back to Europe, and particularly to France. The pendulum which had operated so regularly since the early days of wallpaper craftsmanship was still swinging.

The various excesses to be found in the wallpaper business of the first half of the nineteenth century had their critics even before mechanization was truly under way. J. G. Crace in his lecture on 'The History of Paperhangings' delivered to the Royal Institute of British Architects in 1839, the year of the Potters' first experiments with calico-printing machines, appealed for a better system of art education. Not much later, in 1844, Mawer Cowtan, owner of a wallpaper firm, complained in a lecture to the Decorative Arts Society that designers were paid less than mechanics. The result of such iniquities was a universally poor standard of design. One man who succeeded in relieving the gloom to a large extent was Augustus Welby Pugin, who had collaborated with Crace and Cowtan on the wallpapers for Sir Charles Barry's new Houses of Parliament between 1836 and 1837. Pugin was to have the most profound effect on the next generation of designers, for it was he who pioneered the type of wallpaper that soon became one of the trademarks of the Arts and Crafts Movement. His most important tenet was that wallpaper should be entirely honest about itself, and not try to imitate some other form of decoration or pretend to be three-dimensional. He had a particular love for the Gothic, and this led him to form a company for the production of ornaments in the Gothic style. The company unfortunately went bankrupt, but the feeling it had expressed and consolidated, coupled with

Pugin's strong religious faith, later inspired from him a series of wallpapers of an unwaveringly ecclesiastical and medieval character. This was a feature taken up by many of Pugin's successors. In spite of the great variety of the work produced by the designers who followed in Pugin's wake, all of them adhered to his basic principles. Walls were allowed to appear unashamedly flat, and their function as essential architectural supports was no longer obscured by realistic vines, airy landscapes or other *trompe l'œil* effects.

96
'Tout vient de Dieu', designed by Pugin for S. J. Cooper and produced by Cowtans in collaboration with Crace, 1830–50.
Victoria and Albert Museum, London.

On following pages
Colour 20 *Left*
A decorative scheme by Owen Jones, designed for the billiard room of James Gurney, Regents Park, London, 1870. From a notebook containing original designs by Jones.
Whitworth Art Gallery, University of Manchester.

Colour 21 *Right*
'Blackthorn', intimate yet stately wallpaper by William Morris, printed by Jeffrey & Co., 1892.
Victoria and Albert Museum, London.

130

Among the principal advocates of the new ingenuousness were John Ruskin and Owen Jones. Jones published his views in *The Grammar of Ornament* (1856), a book that was extremely influential not only as a source book of designs but also in its cool, business-like supposition that even in so aesthetic a craft as wallpaper design there was a correct way of doing things. His own preference in wallpaper was for a rather geometrical, formal style, and he utilized the possibilities of turning printing blocks in different directions to produce a mirroring effect. Items in a sketchbook recently identified by Michael Darby of the Victoria and Albert Museum reveal that he was also an excellent colourist (see Colour Plate 20). In 1865 he produced a stunning scheme for the decoration of the Viceroy's Palace at Cairo, with designs based on ornamental devices from Persia. Later he produced a design for a paper with a pilaster motif which was exhibited by Jeffrey and Co. at the 1867 Paris Exhibition. Jones's influence on the wallpaper industry was considerable, as was evinced by the increasing popularity of austere and undemonstrative designs.

Another extremely important person in the world of design at this time was Sir Charles Eastlake. As early as 1836 he was on the Council formed to

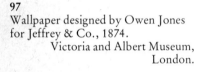

97
Wallpaper designed by Owen Jones for Jeffrey & Co., 1874.
Victoria and Albert Museum, London.

advise the Government on a school of design. He later occupied the posts of Director of the National Gallery and President of the Royal Academy, and enjoyed the support of both Prince Albert and Sir Robert Peel. His nephew Charles Lock Eastlake was equally influential as the author of *Hints on Household Taste* (1872), a book which was to become something of a design bible. In it he sharply criticized the recent styles of wallpaper ('But of all the ugly fashions of that day, by far the most contemptible was that of paperhangings'). Both the ideals which he advocated and the fierce style of their exposition were typical of this particular group of arbiters of taste. The following passage comes from his chapter on the floor and the wall:

> Next to the mistakes committed in the design of carpets, there are few artistic solecisms more apparent than those which the paperstainers perpetrate by way of decoration. Concerning taste, as the old Latin adage informs us, there is no disputing, and if people will prefer a bouquet of flowers or a group of spaniels worked upon the Hearth rug to the conventional patterns which are adopted by the Indian and Turkish weavers, it is difficult to convince them of their error. We require no small amount of art and instruction and experience to see why direct imitation of natural objects is wrong in ornamental design. The quasi-fidelity with which the forms of a rose, or a bunch of ribbons, or a ruined castle, can be produced on carpets, crockery and wallpapers will always possess a certain kind of charm for the uneducated eye, just as the mimicry of natural sounds in music, from the rolling of thunder to the cackling of poultry, will always delight the vulgar ear. Both are ingenious and amusing but neither lie within the legitimate province of art.

Charles L. Eastlake had already adapted some patterns introduced in fourteenth and fifteenth century Italian paintings for use as wallpapers. They were simple diaper designs, that is a pattern completely divided into regular small compartments, and were produced by Woollams. In addition, Eastlake's criticisms had so irritated one manufacturer, Metford Warner of the wallpaper firm Jeffrey & Co., that he had visited Eastlake and persuaded him to design a paper for them, which was called 'Solanum'.

The firm of Jeffrey, Wise & Co. had been founded in 1836, changed its name to Jeffrey, Wise & Horne in 1842, and then again to Horne & Allan in 1843. By 1862 they were known as Jeffrey & Co. and had acquired a high reputation. Following the deaths of the two partners, Edward Hamilton in 1869 and Alfred Brown in 1871, Metford Warner, who had joined the firm in 1866, became the sole proprietor. He continued to direct it until his sons, Marcus and Horace, took over in the 1920s. Arthur Sanderson and Sons acquired the firm's blocks, machines and designs in 1924.

Warner was a significant figure in the wallpaper world. He usefully bridged a gap between the critics and the designers, and although he was active in both these capacities, his most important role was as an intelligent.

98
'Solanum', wallpaper designed by Eastlake, produced by Jeffrey & Co., 1869.

City Art Gallery, Manchester.

On following pages
Colour 22 *Left*
'Pimpernel 82', wallpaper designed by William Morris in 1876, printed by Jeffrey & Co.

Victoria and Albert Museum, London.

Colour 23 *Right*
'Compton 323', wallpaper designed by William Morris in 1895, printed by Jeffrey & Co.

Victoria and Albert Museum, London.

source of encouragement. He gathered together a group of designers of
enormous talent and ran a wallpaper company whose products were
always very skilfully printed. We have already noted that Owen Jones
designed for him. And it was to Metford Warner that William Morris
turned when he found that the technique of wallpaper printing eluded him.

Morris was already closely linked by friendship and coincidence of
interests with the Pre-Raphaelites, who had also dabbled in wallpaper in a
desultory way. Rossetti, for example, wrote in 1860 that he was designing
paper for his drawing room and planned to have it printed both on
common brown packing paper and on blue grocer's paper, to see which
was the better. There is an entry in the account book of Ford Maddox

100
'Chrysanthemum', a fairly
naturalistic wallpaper by Morris,
produced by Jeffrey & Co., 1877.
Victoria and Albert Museum,
London.

Brown for 30 September 1862 'Design for Wallpaper £2'—but as this is a single instance and no examples of his wallpaper design are known, it would seem that his interest was minimal. Of the group it was really only Morris who became seriously interested in designing wallpaper, which he did with unsurpassed skill and fluidity. The first was 'Trellis', designed in 1862 and based on a trellis at the Red House at Bexleyheath in Kent, which the architect Philip Webb had designed for Morris in 1859. (Webb also contributed the birds to the wallpaper.) This was soon followed by 'Daisy', a light, restrained and balanced design, and by 'Fruit'. All three were published in 1864. The actual printing of the wallpapers was one of the few processes with which Morris failed to come to terms successfully.

On following pages
Colour 24 *Left*
Wallpaper frieze designed by Bruce
Talbert in *c.* 1875.
Victoria and Albert Museum,
London.

Colour 25 *Right*
'The Formal Garden', wallpaper
designed by Walter Crane, 1904.
Blockprinted by Jeffrey & Co.
Victoria and Albert Museum,
London.

He abandoned his own attempts with etched zinc plates and production was taken over by Jeffrey and Co. Nevertheless, he closely supervised the printing of his wallpapers (although Metford Warner appears to have won his confidence). The following account appears in a note of Metford Warner's:

> William Morris himself was always at the front, directing, encouraging and forcibly demonstrating as to the incorrigible stupidity of those who did not grasp his ideas. 'Tell them not to improve my colourings' was a message I had to convey to the factory from the master in blue blouse, bare feet in slippers and hands blue from the dye vat.

Although Morris had absorbed the comments of wallpaper critics his papers were rather naively romantic, and they catered respectably for the contemporary taste for naturalism. Even when his work did become formal, it was the formality of the woven textiles which Morris was involved with and studied at the Victoria and Albert Museum, rather than the more geometric formality of, say, Owen Jones. Morris designed in all forty-one wallpapers and five ceiling papers, and his firm produced another forty-one papers besides. What Morris aimed at most commonly in his designs was to reproduce in wallpaper the vigour and logic of plant growth, without directly imitating nature as so many of his contemporaries did. At the same time he maintained that no line or object should be introduced that could not be explained by the structure of the pattern, and was always at pains to conceal his repeats. 'It is important,' he wrote, 'to mask the construction of our patterns enough to prevent people from counting repeats, while we manage to lull their curiosity to trace it out.' (*Some Hints on Pattern Designing* 1881)

The Arts and Crafts Movement, of which Morris was the spiritual leader, produced many fine wallpapers, some of which are still in production today. Although they saw the relentless march of industry as a threat to humanity, and many of them were active socialists believing that good designs should be available to all, the alternative to industry that they pursued could never be a reality for the majority. The wallpapers that they produced remain caviar for an elite, well beyond the means of the general public. Much of the industry thought them a set of amateurs trying to teach real businessmen their trade, but nevertheless their underlying principle—that design should be firstly for men, not profit—survived to become a banner for the Modernists fifty years later.

Also among Metford Warner's designers were William Burges, E. W. Godwin and Albert Moore. Although Burges's papers were popular with architects they were too Gothic to be much appreciated by the public, and they gave rise to the dictum that 'Jeffrey and Co. have gone mad'. There seems also to have been an oriental element in his papers, and one, 'The Daisy and the Snail', is said to have been exhibited in a London industrial exhibition as a Japanese production. The architect E. W. Godwin (who designed the famous 'White House' for the painter Whistler) was also

101
'Christchurch', a less well known
William Morris wallpaper, showing
his skill in masking repeats, produced
by Jeffrey & Co., 1882.
Victoria and Albert Museum,
London.

greatly influenced by the Japanese. The exoticism of his papers is
illustrated by the story of how Godwin arranged to have one of his own
papers hung at his home in his absence but was disappointed on his return
to find that the work had not been done. His housekeeper is said to have
explained: 'Well, did y'ever see such a thing? Why, of course I wasn't going
to have it hung until ye'd seen it.' Like Morris, Godwin seems to have had
cause for complaint about the colours used in the production of his papers,
the inevitable heavy greens gravely reducing the intended effect of his light
and unusual designs.

The Japanese influence, starting in England in the mid 1870s and
featuring particularly strongly in American designs, was by this time

On following pages
Colour 26 Left
Design for a wallpaper by A. F.
Vigers.
Victoria and Albert Museum,
London.

Colour 27 Right
Design in water and body colour for a
wallpaper frieze 'Isis' by C. F. A.
Voysey, c. 1895. Produced by Jeffrey
& Co.
Victoria and Albert Museum,
London.

141

143

102
Japanese lining paper or wallpaper,
c. 1850.
        Victoria and Albert Museum,
                London.

103
Japanese lining or wallpaper, *c.* 1850.
        Victoria and Albert Museum,
                London.

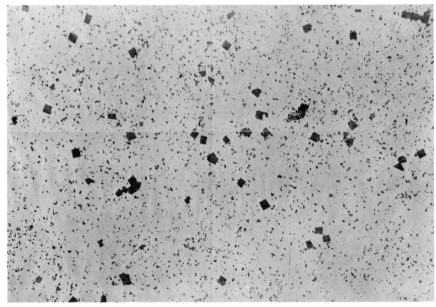

widespread in wallpaper. It had come into its own both directly from Japanese designs and through the filter of the Aesthetic Movement, who adored anything Japanese. A considerable amount of imitation embossed leather wallpaper was imported from Japan, and several artists produced new designs for English versions.

   One man who illustrates the impact of Japanese work in the last quarter of the century is Christopher Dresser, who travelled widely in Europe, Japan and America. Like Morris, however, Dresser often turned more directly to nature (he was, after all, a trained botanist), and there he found

144

104
American wallpaper and frieze in
Japanesque style, produced by
Leissner and Louis in New York,
c. 1875. Unused remnants from a
house in Salem, Oregon where it still
hangs in the parlour. Embossed
machine printed.
  Cooper Hewitt Museum of
  Decorative Arts and Design,
Smithsonian Institution, New York.

the structure and inherent order that he wanted for his designs. Both he and
Godwin worked in the dado-filling-frieze formula which was popular
from about 1870 to 1890. The first wallpaper in this style, produced by
Jeffrey and Co., was apparently a set depicting a cornfield with poppies,
designed by Brightwen Binyon. The dado generally extended about three
feet upwards from floor level, and at the top it was edged with a narrow
paper border or some wood moulding. It was often made of tough, dark
paper, for in this position it would have to take a good deal of wear and
tear. Above it was the filling, separated from the frieze by another paper

106
Design for 'The Sunflower' wallpaper
by Bruce Talbert. Produced by
Jeffrey & Co., 1878.
Victoria and Albert Museum,
London.

border, picture rail or narrow shelf. These divisions were even carried up
the stairs so that specially designed stair wallpapers had to be produced,
stepped and sloping, to cope with the difficulties.

Another prolific and influential designer, much imitated after his early
death, was Bruce J. Talbert, who combined the Japanese feeling of the
time with sympathy for natural forms and for the work of William Morris.
The wallpapers that resulted, picturing stylized, highly decorative yet
entirely recognizable flowers and fruit, were very appealing and popular.
His sunflower series, exhibited at the Paris Universal Exhibition of 1878,
was awarded a gold medal, and received the compliment of being pirated.

It was a conversation with Talbert which prompted Metford Warner to
ask Walter Crane to design a nursery paper. Nursery wallpapers became

extremely popular during the last half of the nineteenth century, and Crane's work as an illustrator of children's books was a ready-made source of motifs and colour schemes. Kate Greenaway, the famous children's illustrator, who is often described with Crane and Randolph Caldecott as one of the 'Academicians of the Nursery', similarly had her work represented in wallpaper form, this time by the firm of David Walker, who chose as his subject her tableaux of the months and seasons of the year.

Crane warned Warner from the start that he must not ask him to design in any particular style, a restriction which proved to be no bother to Warner at all, since from the first paper ('Sing a Song of Sixpence' in 1875) onwards all Crane's work met with great success. Many of his wallpapers showed people and animals, and all are very individualistic, strong and rich. Like Morris, he enjoyed baffling the onlooker—'The more mysteriously you interweave your sprays and stems, the better for your purpose'—but his puzzlingly intricate whirls were often counteracted by soothing and restful colour combinations. His wallpaper carries a heavy burden of symbolism, as we learn from a manufacturer's leaflet accompanying the wallpaper 'Corona Vita':

> Emblematic of a full, rich and ample life not without its changes and contrasts but ever springing anew to flower and fruition. While the floral winged Lions, supporting the Crown of Life, indicate its material Triumphs, the Sphinxes on either side of the tree figure its mystery, and those unanswered problems perpetually presented afresh to humanity in the Fruit of the Tree of Knowledge.

Although he practised well nigh every technique of applied art, including that of leather embossing (his design 'Cupids and Amorini' was produced both in wallpaper and embossed and gilded leather), Crane's wallpaper designs were among his most successful work: 'Margarete', for instance, shown at the Philadelphia Exhibition of 1876, was eulogized by the judges and won a special medal, and his reputation abroad actually exceeded that of Morris. Although he shared many of Morris's Socialist sympathies he differed from him in his attitude to industrialization, urging that art and industry should work in close co-operation. He was closely associated with Morris, collaborating with him on illustrations and being nominated first president of the Arts and Crafts Society, a post to which he returned after Morris's death. It is indicative of the strength of his own sense of design that his work remained very truly his own, despite the proximity of such a powerful personality.

Another important figure in wallpaper design at that time was Lewis F. Day, founder member of the Art Workers Guild, whose members also include several wallpaper designers, Walter Crane among them. Less individualistic than Crane, he was nevertheless an excellent trade designer and very successful. He designed many first-rate very simple wallpapers which could be printed cheaply. He worked for Metford Werner, and was also employed for a time by Simpson's, for whom Jeffreys did the printing.

107 *Above and opposite right*
Two examples of the dado-filling-frieze style. Both produced by Jeffrey & Co. in 1874.
(a) Designed by E. W. Godwin.
(b) Designed by C. Dresser.
Victoria and Albert Museum, London.

But there were dozens of good designers working in wallpaper at this time. Each of the applied arts was benefiting from an unprecedented number of artists who busied themselves with the problems of practical design. This seems to have been partly caused by dissatisfaction with current high-flown ideas about the value and function of art. The members of the Arts and Crafts Movement, feeling that art had become divorced from real life, deliberately turned away from painting and concentrated on work for a wider public. Some credit for the high standard of design should

108 *Left*
Nursery wallpaper by Kate Greenaway illustrating 'The Months', produced by David Walker, *c.* 1893. Machine printed from engraved rollers.
Victoria and Albert Museum, London.

109 *Above left*
'Thys ys ye House thatte Jack Built',
one of Walter Crane's nursery
wallpapers, produced by Jeffrey &
Co., 1886.

Victoria and Albert Museum,
London.

certainly also go to the museums, galleries and art schools which had been
so earnestly opened during the first half of the century.

Work is extant from many of the designers who flourished in this
creative atmosphere. Of special note are Lindsay Butterfield, Joseph
Doran, F. C. Frogatt (who designed for Potters), George Haité (of the
Analgypta Co.), Harry Napper, W. J. Neatby, Walter Tarrant and
Heywood Sumner. Sumner designed wallpapers in the style of Bruce
Talbert and was a prominent member of the Jeffrey and Co. stable.
Jeffreys' designers also included Alan Vigers, whose work was especially
popular (deservedly so, for it has a very pleasant fresh simplicity and
luminosity) and Frederick Vigers, who won the Grand Prize for wallpaper

110 *Left and opposite right*
'Corona Vita', frieze and wallpaper
designed by Crane for Jeffrey & Co.,
1890.

Victoria and Albert Museum,
London.

in the Anglo-French Exhibition of 1908, held at Shepherd's Bush.

Also worthy of note is Arthur Silver whose 'Silver Studio', started in 1880 and finally closed in the 1960s, briefly boasted the assistance not only of Harry Napper but also of Sidney Mawson, a good designer in his own right. Although at the time the Silver Studio was one of the biggest design studios in England, it is now comparatively obscure. But Silver's papers, and to a lesser degree those of his son Rex who took over the firm in later years, certainly deserve to be more widely known, for their patterns, with strong fluid rhythms swaying and bending, are as strong and original as those of many of their contemporaries. Though a friend of Walter Crane and William Morris and influenced to some extent by them both, Silver at

111
Original design for 'Brocade'
wallpaper by L. F. Day, 1885.
 Victoria and Albert Museum,
 London.

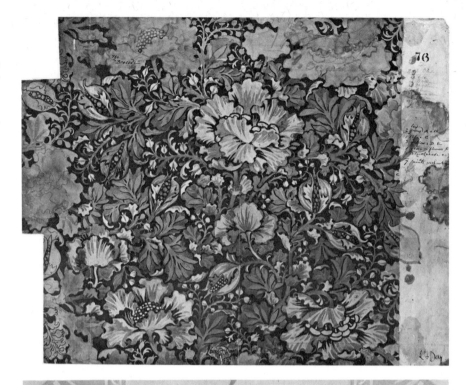

112
Ceiling paper for use with the scheme
'La Margarete', designed by Crane for
Jeffrey & Co., 1876.
 Victoria and Albert Museum,
 London.

152

his best revealed a very individual design sense.

Many of the artists already discussed in this chapter would today be labelled Art Nouveau, though it was a term which many of them found abhorrent in its connotations of decadence. An extract from *The Masque of the Edwards of England*, written by C. R. Ashbee, founder of the Guild of Handicraft in 1881, neatly summarizes one view of the style:

114
Modern reprint of a design by L. F. Day, *c.*1890.
Whitworth Art Gallery, University of Manchester.

113
'The Garden Arbor' wallpaper designed by Heywood Sumner in the last quarter of the nineteenth century.
Whitworth Art Gallery, University of Manchester.

115
'Monkshood', wallpaper designed by
Alan F. Vigers in the last quarter of
the nineteenth century.
Whitworth Art Gallery,
University of Manchester.

116
'Columbine', wallpaper designed by
A. F. Vigers in 1901. Produced by
Jeffrey & Co. Colour print from
wood blocks.
Victoria and Albert Museum,
London.

117 *Opposite*
A wallpaper frieze designed by the
Silver Studio, 1902.
Victoria and Albert Museum,
London.

I'm in the fashion—non controversial
And the fashion is nothing if not commercial
Pre-Raphaelite once, with a tiny twist
Of the philosophical Hedonist
Inspired by Whistler—next a touch
Of the 'Arts and Crafts' but not too much,
Then Impressionism, the daintiest fluke;
Then the German squirm, and the Glasgow spook,
A spice of the latest French erotic
Anything new and Studiotic
As long as it tells in black and white
and however wrong comes out all right
'Id est', as long as it pays you know,
That's what's meant by Art Nouveau!

The origins of Art Nouveau are many and complex and fall well outside the scope of this book. But among the first designers wholly to convert their style to the Art Nouveau objectives of 'symbolic patterning, curvilinear motif and structural simplicity'* were Arthur Heygate Mackmurdo and his friend, fellow architect and partner in the Century Guild Herbert Horne, both of whom designed wallpapers. It has recently been suggested in an article by Malcolm Haslam† that Mackmurdo's attendances at lectures on marine biology, given by the Darwinist T. H. Huxley at the South Kensington Museum, may have stimulated the undulant sea-plant designs that were one of this artist's favourite motifs. Such devices, and the flowing manner in which they were executed, were later to become one of the major elements in Art Nouveau.

In France there had been very little progress in wallpaper design since the peak reached at the beginning of the nineteenth century. Manufacturers urged by their critics to look for better quality turned back to old textile designs and produced imitations. Paul Balin's designs, for instance, typify a backward-looking fussiness which his admiration for the Arts and Crafts Movement could not shift. Metford Warner said of them 'Some of the most beautiful paperhangings ever produced being those printed and embossed by M. Balin, still they after all bring no credit to the designer of this day.' Art Nouveau, however, brought something substantial and new which Europe could adapt and alter to its own tastes. Samuel Bing, founder of the Paris shop La Maison de l'Art Nouveau gave full credit: 'When English creations began to appear, a cry of delight sounded throughout Europe. Its echo can still be heard in every country.'

In America, the visits of many of the well-known English designers had precipitated great interest in the Arts and Crafts Movement. Many designs were bought from English artists, or failing that, they were emulated or even pirated. No American designers however stand out as breaking new ground. Neither was there such a warm reaction to Art Nouveau as there was in France. New inspiration for American design came with the

118
Wallpaper designed by A. H. Mackmurdo for the Century Guild, c. 1884.

Victoria and Albert Museum, London.

* Mario Amaya *Art Nouveau* Studio Vista, London, and Dutton, New York, 1966

† *Country Life* 6 March 1975, pp.574–9

119
A sheet of French borders designed by
Paul Balin, (active around 1863, died
1898), copies of woven materials,
produced in flock.
Victoria and Albert Museum,
London.

functionalism of the Modern Movement of the early twentieth century, a
functionalism which, although it shared many of the basic ideals of the Arts
and Crafts Movement, was very different in its methods and results.

While France was still absorbing Art Nouveau and America was on the
verge of discovering functionalism, England was beginning to go through
the phases that culminated eventually its own, rather insipid, form of
Modernism. One figure who links many of the styles, and in a way bridges
the two centuries, is the architect C. F. A. Voysey, who began designing
wallpapers in 1884 and continued until 1930. He was initiated into
wallpaper design by his friend Mackmurdo and was at first strongly

influenced by him, turning to him for practical advice on the shading of
colours for example. He was also, inevitably, influenced by Morris, but so
strict were his architectural principles of 'flatness' for wallpaper design that
his work always retains a strong structural feeling. He used wallpaper in a
more limited way than Morris, preferring to restrict its use to bedrooms,
and favouring low friezes with the wall-space above them painted white.
He differed from Morris too in that he had no desire to disguise his repeats.
After 1900 his style matured into a completely individual, calm, quiet and
decisive manner which could absorb fresh subject matter and treat it in an

160

individual way: 'Squire's Garden' is an excellent example. After the First World War, Voysey's production slackened off, and his development came to a halt. From then on he was content to issue reprints of earlier designs. The bird motifs, particularly owls, which had become so dear to him, were characteristic of the rather whimsical and fantastical element in which he indulged after his retirement from architecture. But before this paralysis set in, he wrote an article for the *Journal of Decorative Arts* in 1904 which lamented the way Art Nouveau had turned out and looked forward—with, alas, rather inaccurate prophecy—to a new age of perfection in wallpaper design:

> I think the condition which has made Art Nouveau possible is a distinctly healthy development, but at the same time the manifestation of it is distinctly unhealthy and revolting . . . what we need now is more religious earnestness and conscientiousness, and a real style will in the end result from it.

122 *Opposite*
'The Squire's Garden', wallpaper designed by Voysey, 1898. Surface machine printed.
Whitworth Art Gallery,
University of Manchester.

Back to White

IF one may generalize for a moment, it could be said that there were two major elements in English wallpaper design at the turn of this century. The Arts and Crafts Movement was still enormously influential, but it had lost some of its initial quality and dynamism with the death of its leading exponent William Morris. Secondly there was Art Nouveau, a vogue which rapidly became over-commercialized, yet caught the imagination of many designers, especially in Europe, and precipitated the new burst of interest in design which swept through France and Germany and their neighbours during the first quarter of the century. The picture was blurred by numerous cross-currents of influence, such as that of the Aesthetic Movement, which lost its main impetus by about the late eighties but remained as a source of ideas and styles for some times afterwards. The English wallpaper scene was a shifting and confused one, but for many people abroad London was still decidedly the centre of the decorative arts. Continental and American designers turned for inspiration to the work of Morris, Crane, Mackmurdo and Voysey and their contemporaries. Germany went so far as to send a representative to report on English housing in all its aspects. This was Hermann Muthesius, who in 1898 gave a first-hand impression of Ashbee's Guild and School of Handicraft in the German magazine *Dekorative Kunst,* and in the following years brought out several illustrated volumes on contemporary English housing.

In Continental Europe there rapidly occurred a vigorous flowering of the Art Nouveau style, principally in France and Belgium but also notably in Munich and Vienna. The Wiener Werkstätten, founded in 1903 by the architect Josef Hoffman, developed an austere rectilinear style, very different from the undulating Art Nouveau motifs favoured by the French. The best known wallpaper designer of this group is Dagobert Peche (Colour Plate 28), who produced some fine papers in the twenties. The earlier work of the Czech designer Alphons Mucha (Colour Plate 29), on the other hand, is characterized by strong, simple lines and fluid swirls. Best known for his posters commissioned by Sarah Bernhardt, he also did designs for wallpapers, and some are illustrated in his book *Documents Décoratifs,* published in 1902 to advertise his ideas on all aspects of decorative art. They appear not to have been produced however. He seems

not to have thought of his 'decorative panels' as wallpaper; but certainly panels that were stylistically and structurally not far from Mucha's had been produced specifically as wallpaper. Dufour's panels (see Plate 67) are examples of this.

In Germany in 1907 the first Deutscher Werkbund was formed by Muthesius and his disciples. Unlike the British guilds and crafts societies of the nineteenth century the Werkbund included not only artists, but also manufacturers. They took a positive line on industrialization. At their first Annual Meeting they stated that 'There is no fixed boundary line between the tool and the machine . . . It is not the machines themselves that make work inferior, but our inability to use them properly.'* The first Werkbund was formed in 1907, and between 1910 and 1917 parallel Werkbunds were established in Austria, Switzerland and Sweden.

There were several outstanding wallpaper designers connected with the Werkbunds. Notable among them are Georges Lemmen, whose work forms a link between designs based on nature and a more linear style, and who with Van de Velde designed the interior of the Maison Bing; Van de

123
Voysey room, showing his ideas in the use of wallpaper with a low white frieze, and many Art Nouveau artefacts.
Geffrye Museum, London.

* Quoted from Nikolaus Pevsner *Pioneers of Modern Design* Penguin Books, Harmondsworth 1960

164

Velde himself; Walter Leistikow, whose Art Nouveau interests were tempered with the restraint of the Japanese; and Otto Eckmann. These last two showed a particular interest in the possibilities of the frieze, an element which was also to capture the attention of English designers for more than two decades. 1919 saw the founding in Weimar of the Bauhaus. This movement which was to become of such great importance in twentieth century creative design was for wallpaper something of a negative influence. Wallpaper could have no place in the streamlined, practical and industrial world that the Bauhaus advocated.

124 *Opposite*
'Narcissus', German wallpaper in the Art Nouveau style, designed by A. O. Verneuil for the firm of Engelhard, Mannheim in 1900.
Deutsches Tapetenmuseum, Kassel.

125
'The Nettles', *c.* 1922, designed by Atelier Martine, printed by Paul Dumas, Paris.
Bibliothèque Forney, Paris.

126
Advertisement for a Swedish wallpaper factory, *c.* 1900.
Nordiska Museet, Stockholm.

'Poppies' *c.* 1912 designed by Atelier Martine, printed by Paul Dumas, Paris.

Bibliothèque Forney, Paris.

In 1910 in Vienna the French fashion designer Paul Poiret had met Josef Hoffmann and visited the school attached to the Wiener Werkstätten. He was impressed by the idea of a school of decorative art for children, but disliked the rigid discipline under which the pupils worked. In 1912 he started a school of decorative design in his own house in Paris, offering a small wage, lunch and tea to his young students, all girls aged about twelve, from working-class backgrounds. He allowed them to develop their talents quite freely, limiting his interference to taking them on visits to zoos and parks. The designs produced by the girls of this school, which Poiret called the Atelier Martine, were sometimes transcribed into wallpaper

designs, for which Poiret would pay a bonus. Before long a shop, the
Maison Martine, was opened to sell the wallpapers and other articles the
school produced, and the venture met with an enormous success.

Working at the same time in France were André Groult, who, with
André Mare, decorated the house of the artist Raymond Duchamp-Villon,
and Paul Follot. Both were at first associated with La Maison Moderne, a
group concerned with the inexpensive production of Art Nouveau

128
'The Tennis Players', c. 1925, designed
by Mme de Andrada, printed by Paul
Dumas, Paris.
    Bibliothèque Forney, Paris.

artefacts. Later the men reacted against Art Nouveau, and were to go down in design history as among the progenitors of the movement known, after the 1925 Exposition des Arts Décoratifs, as Art Deco. André Groult became interested in wallpaper design in about 1912 and founded a firm which employed the talents of Laboureur and the painter Marie Laurencin. The enterprise was eventually taken over by Hans et Fils, who closed down in 1969 but still retain the blocks and catalogues.

The bright colours and *joie de vivre* of the new French styles were the very antithesis of the restrained work which was coming from Germany. To some extent, however, the designs of the two countries came closer together when Cubism began to influence French wallpapers and Art Deco lost some of its exuberance. A Cubist predilection for straight lines can be seen, for instance, in the work of Paul Véra and Henri Stéphany (Colour Plates 31, 32).

In the thirties silkscreen printing began to be used for wallpaper production. At this time also the firm Nobilis was beginning to produce wallpaper by the *pochoir* method, a combination of ordinary stencilling and collotype printing. Collotype is similar to silkscreen printing in that a gelatine coating is rendered light-sensitive, but the coat is spread on a sheet of glass rather than on a fabric screen. When the coat is dry a photographic negative is placed on the glass and exposed to light. The gelatine is hardened in proportion to the amount of light passing through the negative, and becomes capable of accepting the printing ink. The unexposed areas are kept damp during the printing process to repel the ink. An extremely fine gradation in tone can be achieved by this method. Silk screening is not suitable for printing large quantities, since the life of the screen is obviously much shorter than that of a wood block, but it can be used very successfully for short-run and experimental work.

Across the Channel by this time, wallpaper had for decades been undergoing a comparatively barren period. By the First World War wallpaper designs in England had lost all the vitality of the end of the nineteenth century. The amalgamation of the English wallpaper manufacturers in 1899 had had particularly unfortunate results in this respect. The schism between, on the one hand, a huge mechanized organization and, on the other, a smaller number of individual designers, did nothing to benefit either group. The war of course slowed the development of the decorative arts in all European countries, but it was England, lacking native design vitality in any case, that seemed to ride the troubles least successfully. It was decided that it was not in the country's interests to issue new books of wallpaper designs, and short time was started in the factories. Coal tar dyes (supplied by Germany) became scarce, and paper supply and quality dropped rapidly, so that even the halved demand of wartime could not be met. It was soon discovered however that the old Anaglypta presses could forge shell bodies, and the newly formed Wallpaper Manufacturers went to war.

Colour 28 *Opposite*
Two German wallpapers designed by Dagobert Peche for the firm of Flammersheim and Steinmann, Köln, 1924–5.
Deutsches Tapetenmuseum, Kassel.

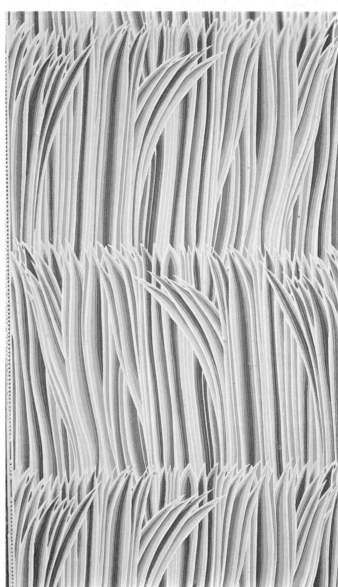

169

129
'The Bathers', designed by Paul Véra before 1925, printed from wood blocks.

130 *Opposite*
Three English friezes.
(a) 'Africa' frieze by J. Wood, 1913.
(b) 'Osiris' frieze by J. Wood, 1907.
(c) 'Shaftesbury' frieze by G. F. Jackson, 1907.
             Whitworth Art Gallery,
             University of Manchester.

On following pages
Colour 29 *Left*
Design for wallpaper and frieze by A. Mucha. Plate 38 of *Documents Décoratifs*, 1902.
             Victoria and Albert Museum,
             London.
Colour 30 *Right*
Wallpaper designed by Raubenheimer for J. Strauven, Bonn, 1928. It is in the possession of the firm.
   Deutsches Tapetenmuseum, Kassel.

131
Frieze designed by Mabel Lucy
Atwell with scenes from nursery tales.
Printed by C. & J. G. Potter,
Darwen, 1913.
        Victoria and Albert Museum,
                London.

132
Two English scenic friezes.
(a) Landscape frieze, designed by
    Covillot, produced by Allan,
    Cockshut and Co., 1907.
(b) The *Surf* frieze, designed by G.
    Pretty, 1913.
        Whitworth Art Gallery,
        University of Manchester.

There was one development in English wallpaper design which may have been influenced by the German designers already mentioned or may have grown from the dado-filling-frieze phenomenon of the late nineteenth century. The difficulty of obtaining plentiful materials may also have been an influence. Whatever the causes, the simple result was the development of the frieze, in a quite remarkable and insular way. It was used to enliven painted walls or dull paper of poor quality. Much imagination was used in both subject matter and methods of production, and a most varied and prolific style soon emerged.

133
'The Apple Tree', a 'Crown Design' by Sidney Haward, c. 1910.
Whitworth Art Gallery,
University of Manchester.

One aspect of the frieze vogue was a liking for 'crown' designs. These consisted of frieze and filling together, produced either in the usual way as a vertical strip or in horizontal strips about four yards long. They were generally floral. There was also an air of romanticism in British design, and a touch of escapism, which was manifested in either idyllic, idealized landscapes featured in some of the friezes and in papers like 'Castle with Foxgloves' or in the glamour of 'Coastal Resort at Night' or in distant historical and geographical motifs. The discovery of the tomb of Tutankhamun provided the stimulus for some Egyptian-style wallpapers.

134
'The Orchard', designed by W. J. Neatby, produced by Jeffrey & Co., c. 1904.

Whitworth Art Gallery, University of Manchester.

Colour 31 *Opposite*
Wallpaper designed by Henri Stéphany, c. 1925.

On following pages
Colour 32 *Left*
'Arabian Constructions', designed by Henri Stéphany, printed by Follot, Paris, 1928.

Colour 33 *Right*
'The Cupid's Dial' frieze produced by Chappel and Payne, London, 1915.
Victoria and Albert Museum, London.

135
Two panels of English romantic
wallpaper produced by John Line and
Sons.
(a) 'Castle with Foxgloves', *c.* 1926.
(b) 'The Chiltern Decoration', in use
1926.

Whitworth Art Gallery,
University of Manchester.

136
'Coastal Resort at Night', English
wallpaper showing a Hollywood
influence. Produced by John Line and
Sons, London, during the 1930s.
Whitworth Art Gallery,
University of Manchester.

On following pages
Colour 34 *Above left*
Frieze showing the continuing
interest in Chinoiserie, produced by
John Line and Sons, *c*. 1930. The
rectangles at top and bottom are
reminiscent of moving film stock.
Whitworth Art Gallery,
University of Manchester.

Colour 35 *Below left*
Panel of flock wallpaper, possibly
depicting a 'glass tree' for which there
was a vogue in the 1920s. Black was
also fashionable on walls at the time.
Produced by John Line and Sons, in
use 1924.
Whitworth Art Gallery,
University of Manchester.

Colour 36 *Above right*
Photographic scenic wallpaper
produced by Brepols
Behangselpapieren, Turnhout, 1974.
Groupement des Fabricants
de Papiers Peints de Belgique.

Colour 37 *Below right*
Floral wallpaper produced by Les
Papeteries de Genval, 1975.
Groupement des Fabricants
de Papiers Peints de Belgique.

Chinoiserie enjoyed a new fashion while model ships and glass or semi-precious stone imitation miniature trees, all popular in both England and America, provided new and well-liked themes (see Colour Plate 35).

The cut-out motif, as used in the Egyptian-style paper, enjoyed a prodigious vogue. Many houses had fields of paper tulips arising from their skirting boards and sprays of paper autumn leaves radiating from each corner. Decorative panels, until now generally rectangular, were trimmed and shaped. Wallpaper octagons, circles and lunettes strategically placed, perhaps above the sideboard, became common features of decoration.

137
Textured plain paper with appliqué motifs in an Egyptian style, though possibly depicting Tarzan. Produced by John Line and Sons, London, in use 1934.

Whitworth Art Gallery,
University of Manchester.

138
Galleon panel produced by John Line and Sons, in use 1932.

Whitworth Art Gallery,
University of Manchester.

184

American designers were at this time beginning to come into their own, but they were very much in the tradition of the plain-wall advocates. The strongest design influence was America's band of very progressive architects, and of them only Frank Lloyd Wright is known to have produced wallpaper.

In America, as in England, the lack of financial security for everyone meant that both individual designers and large companies were unwilling to take risks. A vague pseudo-historical style developed in both furniture and wallpapers which in its fear of displeasing the public was similar to the insipid porridge papers provided for the friezes.

The British exhibits at the long awaited Paris Exhibition of Decorative Arts in 1925 were half-hearted. America did not exhibit at all, for it was felt that they simply had no work to put forward. The Metropolitan Museum, however, showed some of the work which had been featured in the Paris Exhibition a year later in New York, and in 1927 there was an important exhibition of Swedish design and several big stores arranged exhibitions of international decorative art. Later, in 1939, from May to October, the Cooper Hewitt Museum in New York held an exhibition of wallpaper design and production to celebrate the bicentenary of the beginning of manufacture of wallpaper in America. Its ambition was to convey 'the importance of wallpaper as a medium for retaining the spirit of handicraft in an age of mass production'.

Both England and America, now convinced that they were design slums, both dogged by the Depression and the looming threat of the Second World War, continued to produce not a radical movement in decorative design but scattered work of an individualistic and whimsical

139
An example of the shaped wallpaper panel, a river scene with a punt. Lunette produced by John Line and Sons, in use 1932.
Whitworth Art Gallery,
University of Manchester.

140
'Design 602', wallpaper designed by
Frank Lloyd Wright for F.
Schumacher & Co., New York, in
1956. Handprinted from the Taliesin
Line.
Victoria and Albert Museum,
London.

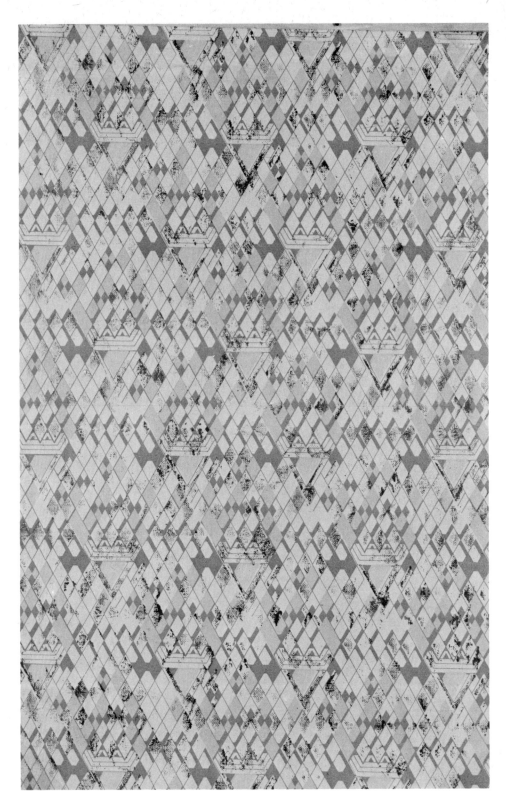

141
'Rhododendron', wallpaper of the typical blurry texture of the late twenties, designed by A. J. Baker for Potters, Darwen, 1929.
Whitworth Art Gallery, University of Manchester.

142
Drawings on paper by Eric Gill, in a white outline on charcoal grey paper for the sitting room of Oliver Hill, English, 1938.

143
'Camels and Sanddunes', an 'amusing' lithograph wallpaper designed by Edward Bawden, English, 1931.
Victoria and Albert Museum, London.

nature. Basil Ionides in his book *Colour and Interior Decoration*, published in 1926, discusses oddities like the use on walls of brown wrapping paper edged with gilt borders, and silver paper in bathrooms. Eric Gill's work, mural in quality yet executed on paper and therefore just within the confines of wallpaper in its broadest sense, shows one of the few examples of a combination of Modernist influence with the rather quirky quality in English decoration. There was little understanding in England or America of movements on the Continent. Even good designers like Edward Bawden and John Aldridge in England, and Ilonka Karasz in America, sometimes had a jokey feeling in their designs which could not have been found in either France or Germany, or in the Scandinavian countries which were beginning to enter wallpaper production in earnest.

There was the same unadventurousness in furniture design. The reluctance to admit anything other than reproduction antique furniture into the shops was weakened during the thirties by the work of Serge Chermayeff who had married into the furnishing firm of Waring and Gillow, and who, with the help of Paul Follot, held an exhibition of Modern French and English Decoration in 1928, which received great praise and filled English designers with renewed enthusiasm. Improvements were, however, only apparent in the work of a few people, often jobless artists and architects driven into interior decoration by financial distress. Their work was not generally to be found in shops.

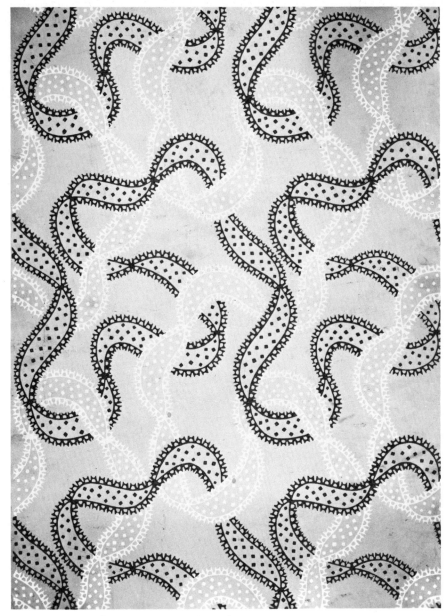

144
'Lace', wallpaper designed by John
Aldridge, English, 1939.
Victoria and Albert Museum,
London.

A new influence was felt in England and America before the war: that of
Scandinavia. Although production of wallpaper started late in Scandinavia
it began to be used extensively there, and a series of competitions were held
in wallpaper design. The designs produced fell on the whole into two
types, those on a small scale providing an all-over effect and those with a
dominating pattern of large motifs. Papers of the second category were
often used on only one wall, and some schemes combined the two types
very successfully to emphasize the spatial characteristics of the rooms. At
this point, the movement for plain painted walls gained a new advocate in

145
'Serenade', an American mezzotone
wallpaper designed by Ilonka Karasz,
seen here in the bedroom of William
Katzenbach at Sneden's Landing,
New York. Produced by some form
of screen printing, 1930–50.
Katzenbach & Warren Inc.,
New York.

Le Corbusier. He had produced a range of wallpapers called 'Claviers de Couleurs' for the Swiss firm Salubra in about 1932. Many of the papers were entirely plain, just carefully chosen colours, though some had slightly irregular white dots, one showed a white trellis on blue, and some papers were slightly grained; they bore the rather romantic titles of 'Space', 'Sky', 'Velvet', 'Scenery', 'Sound'. Corbusier headed the catalogue with a quotation from Fernand Léger—'L'homme a besoin de couleur pour vivre; c'est un element aussi necessaire que l'eau ou le feu' ('Man needs colour to live; it is an element as necessary as water or fire'). Later, however, he was to turn to white as morally the best colour for walls. In his *Decorative Art Today* he says:

Imagine the effect of The Law of Ripolin [an internationally known paint which is still in production]. Every citizen is obliged to replace his hangings, his damask, his wallpapers, his stencils, with a layer of pure white Ripolin. You are bringing cleanliness into your own house: everything shows itself as it is. Then you clean inside yourself, for you will start refusing to admit anything which is not licit, authorized, wanted, desired or conceived: you only act once you have conceived an idea. When shadows and dark corners surround you, you are only at home as far as the blurred edges of the obscure areas.

After this statement even fewer of the contemporary artists and designers were inspired to take much interest in the production of wallpaper. Ironically, the plan for the central business district of Le Corbusier's *Ville Radieuse* has since been reproduced as a wallpaper.

With the exigencies of the Second World War the wallpaper industry in many countries slowed, but of necessity design research was carried out into economic and functional artefacts. The Utility furniture of Britain was one result of this. Immediately after the war, especially in Britain and America, exhibitions of decorative art were organized as part of a big drive to boost morale and start back along the road to economic stability. One of the first was that held at the Suffolk Galleries, Pall Mall, London, by the Central Institute of Art and Design for the British Wallpaper Industry. The hopes for a brave new world and the belief in educating the public caused cross-currents of influence, design councils, a spate of new design magazines—and the Festival of Britain. A great admiration for Scandinavian design brought an added spaciousness and boldness to the design of British wallpapers.

Artists were no longer so dismissive of wallpaper, and among others Graham Sutherland and John Minton both produced wallpaper designs. More important however were the professional designers at work in England during the fifties and sixties, many of them displaying the influence of printed textiles, with which they were principally concerned. Among them were Roger Nicolson, Lucienne Day and the youthful group who produced the well-known 'Palladio' range (whose members included Natalie Gibson and the fashion designer Zandra Rhodes).

Germany too turned to its professional artists and art schools and
collaborated with students to produce new collections such as 'Krefeld
Artwerk' (the work of a class at Krefeld Art School under the supervision
of Gerhard Kradow, who had been a pupil of Paul Klee and Wassily
Kandinsky at the Bauhaus), and the collection 'Neue Wohnung' designed
by the Werkakademie of Kassel with their lecturer Leistikow.

For good or ill, another element in wallpaper design which gained
ground in the 1930s and is still very important is the reproduction of
historic papers. The most popular designs have been those taken from
British wallpapers of the last century; many of the names found in the last
chapter can also be found in contemporary wallpaper catalogues. In
America in particular reproductions are big business, with wallpaper firms
producing not only reprints of nineteenth century papers but also copies of
early French and English imported papers, and of Chinese wallpapers, the
Chinese copies often handpainted.

Recent developments have been the introduction of vinyl wallpapers,
which after an initial boom have fallen off in popularity, and the use of
photography in designing wallpapers. The 'Optacor' collection, by the
Marburg factory, produced in 1970–71, is a good example. Slivers of stone

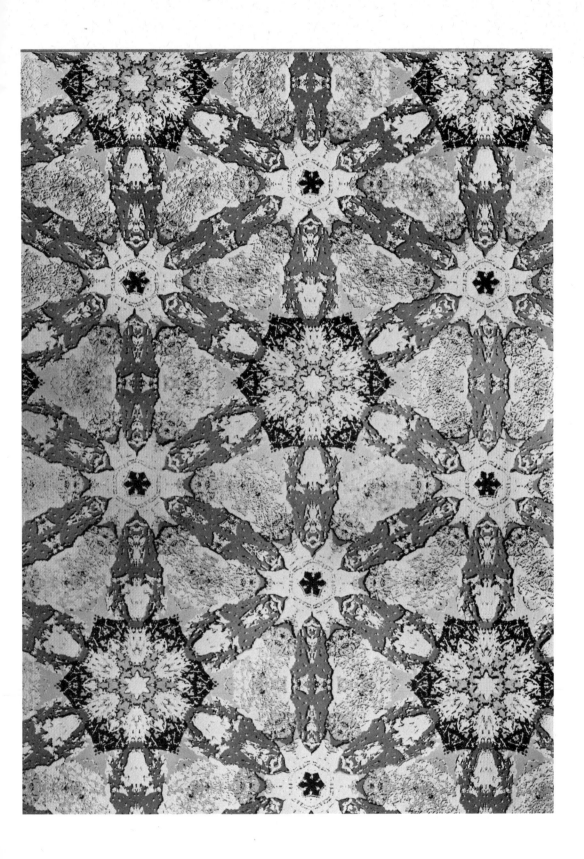

'Oh Promised Land—oh sweet
Freedom', American wallpaper
designed by Jack Denst, *c.*1968, and
produced by Jack Denst Designs, Inc.
Victoria and Albert Museum,
London.

have been photographed microscopically, using polarized light, and the photographs arranged into a repeating design by the studio staff. Photography has also been recently used more directly by wallpaper firms (see Colour Plate 36).

The paper mural type of design still has a corner of the market—the work of Jack Denst is an example. Possibly the recent vogue for pop and pin-up posters or even large bill posters as interior wall decoration should

149
'Trains', handprinted wallpaper designed by Saul Steinberg for Piazza Prints, c. 1950.
Victoria and Albert Museum, London.

be included in a study of wallpapers, for these are, after all, in the tradition of decorative panels, started by the *dominotiers* and carried through the history of wallpaper.

It is now almost impossible to distinguish the nationality of any design and there seems to be a general trend to somewhat large, brash patterns. The majority of wallpapers are produced by vast and impersonal industries, often using the talents of their own staff designers. On the other hand there are increasing numbers of small firms who can oversee the whole production with a far more direct interest and a fresher approach.

150
'Ophelia', a recent wallpaper printed on a silver ground.
Osborne and Little, London.

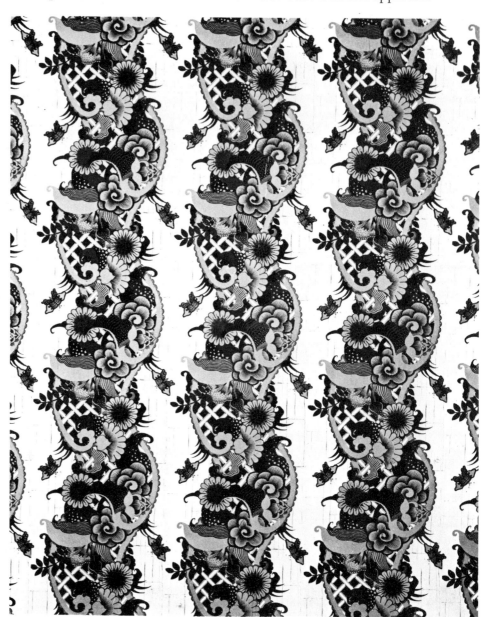

151 *Opposite*
'Koh-i-nor', a modern small motif wallpaper by Osborne and Little.
Council of Industrial Design, London.

197

Some of these small firms are also involved in fashion or textiles and utilize the same blocks or screens for both fabric and paper. Many use simple motifs, often very small ones, and they are also commonly influenced by the designs of Morris, Crane, Day and Voysey and other designers of the late nineteenth century. With the cost of both materials and production now running very high perhaps the frieze or appliqué motifs of the early twentieth century will return to favour providing a quick and economical change of decor especially for those who dislike the all-over pattern of conventional wallpaper. A firm specializing in friezes has recently been established in London; also, some excellent simple and bold friezes have been designed to combine with plain coloured papers. The age-old relationship between wallpaper and other mural coverings continues. Hessians, corks and felts can all be bought as 'wallpaper', and metallicized papers, a distant relative of embossed and gilded leather hangings and the latest example of the wallpaper makers' continuing fascination with shine, are also popular. In some cases the quality of a silver ground to the wallpaper design has the effect of apparently completely removing the wall and leaving a lacework of pattern through which the observer can see reflections. Such designs are produced by Osborne and Little, whose thoughtful experiments and strong designs make them one of the most interesting wallpaper producers at the moment, and must surely give them a secure place in future histories of wallpaper.

The fashion for plain painted walls, although still safe good taste, is a little unexciting. One wonders when a new movement in wallpaper will grow out of the technical developments and the independence of today's young designers.

Appendix: Uncovering Wallpaper

UNCOVERING old wallpaper, often layer upon layer of it, is a common experience; anyone who has been involved in redecorating or structural alterations is bound to have found, be it with interest or irritation, evidence of past styles, fragments or whole walls of wallpaper of the past, whether distant or recent. Large areas of old paper in good condition (although comparatively uncommon) are still discovered, and if you feel that such a find may be of historic value, it would be advisable to contact a museum for advice on conservation, removal and remounting. There are some commercial firms, mainly American, which will undertake this work.

A likely place to find very old wallpaper is under woodwork which has been added at a later date to a building of the sixteenth, seventeenth, eighteenth or early nineteenth centuries. This includes door jambs, skirting boards etc., as well as wood panelling. In some cases papers have been discovered underneath a coat of plaster, which fortunately peels off quite easily.

The existing woodwork may once have been edged with decorative paper borders; these quite often survive although the rest of the wallpaper may have been stripped off, or as with the Victorian 'dado-filling-frieze' type of decoration may indicate that there are different types of designs to be found at different places and levels throughout the room. Ceilings too may have a centrepiece or corners as well as or instead of an all-over decorative paper.

It is good policy to record your find before tampering with it. Old wallpaper is very brittle and attempts to move it may not meet with success. Colour photographs or coloured drawings or tracings will retain information and lessen disappointment. Fortunately, old glue loses much of its adhesive powers, so with patience and a flat-bladed knife of some sort a good deal can often be achieved. The first (bottom) paper can frequently be eased off in quite large sheets by inserting the knife between it and the plaster. Wallpaper stuck direct on to wood will not come away in this fashion; if it is at all possible it would be far better to remove the whole thing—wood and wallpaper complete. Do not attempt to roll any old wallpapers, which would almost certainly crack, try to keep them flat.

Smallish fragments can be treated like drawings and mounted between sheets of card, though it is better to keep wallpaper samples out of bright light, as they may well fade.

It is quite likely that after working the paper off the wall, you will have a 'wallpaper sandwich'—many layers still firmly stuck together. These can often be steamed apart. Catherine Frangiamore of the Cooper Hewitt Museum New York recommends the use of a small hand-held steamer of the type which will produce a concentrated point of steam for use on a small area. Failing that, briefly soak the papers in lukewarm water. The solubility of glue often only just anticipates the solubility of the colours used in printing. Thus it is imperative that a careful watch be kept on the material and the separated layers removed as soon as possible. It is important to have something on which to place the layers one by one, something to which they will not stick—tin foil, waxed paper, or a wire screen for example.

Wallpaper can be steamed or moistened for removal from the wall but this really requires two people, one to steam and one to support the paper as it falls away from the wall. Again a suitable receptacle must be ready. Should the glue prove non-water soluble it will be a case of trial and error with other solvents on the edges of the paper.

Soaking, and to some degree steaming, is likely to cause the colours to fade somewhat and it is probable that the colours will already be greatly altered from their original. Nevertheless old wallpapers are often of interest and delight to those who find them, giving an insight, no matter how slight, into history.

Firms which conserve wallpaper on a commercial basis:
    (This list is from The Association for Preservation Technology Newsletter No. II Vol. II, and was supplied by Catherine Lynn Frangiamore of the Cooper Hewitt Museum of Decorative Arts and Design, Smithsonian Institution.)
A. L. Diament & Co., 2415 South Street, Philadelphia, Pa. 19146 & 969 Third Avenue, New York, N.Y. 10022
Charles R. Gracie and Sons Inc., 979 Third Avenue, New York, N.Y. 10022
Guertler Studies, 245 East 84th Street, New York, N.Y. 10028
Nancy McClelland Inc., 232 East 59th Street, New York, N.Y. 10022
Watson and Collin, 168 East 91st Street, New York, N.Y. 10028

Bibliography

Ackerman, Phyllis *Wallpaper, its History, Design and Use* London 1923

Aslin, Elizabeth *The Aesthetic Movement: Prelude to Art Nouveau* Paul Elek, London 1969 and Praeger, New York 1969

Battersby, Martin *The Decorative Twenties* Studio Vista, London 1969 and Walker, New York 1969

   The Decorative Thirties Studio Vista, London 1971 and Walker, New York 1971

Bock, Judith *The Wallpaper Designs of Voysey* 1966

Brunhammer, Yvonne *The Nineteen-Twenties Style* Tudor, New York 1969

   Cento Legni Remondiani Museo Civico di Bassano del Grappa, Italy 1959

Clouzot, H., and Chas. Follot *Histoire du papier peint en France* Paris 1935

Colby, Averil *Samplers* Batsford, London 1964 and Branford, Newton Centre, Mass. 1965

Crace, J. G. 'A History of Paperhangings', lecture delivered to Royal Institute of British Architects, Feb. 1839

Cramm, Ralph Adams *Impressions of Japanese Architecture* New York 1905

Deutsches Tapetenmuseum Catalogue, Kassel 1955

Dossie, R. *Handmaid to the Arts* London 1758

Dresser, Christopher *Japan, its Architecture, Art and Art Manufactures* London 1882

Eastlake, Sir Charles Lock *Hints on Household Taste in Furniture, Upholstery and Other Details* London 1872; reprinted Dover, New York 1970 and Gregg International, Farnborough 1972

Entwisle, E. A. *The Book of Wallpaper* London 1954; reprinted Kingsmead, Bath 1970

   French Scenic Wallpapers, 1810–1850 F. Lewis, Leigh-on-Sea 1972

   The Literary History of Wallpaper Batsford, London 1960

   Wallpapers of the Victorian Era F. Lewis, Leigh-on-Sea 1964 and Textile Book Service, Metuchen, N.J. 1964

Entwisle, E. A. and A. V. Sugden *The Potters of Darwen* 1939
   Notes on 'A History of Paperhanging' by J. G. Crace Birmingham 1939
Floud, Peter *The Wallpaper Designs of William Morris* 1960
Foley, E. *Book of Decorative Furniture* vol. 1, London 1910
Frangiamore, Catherine Lynn 'Wallpapers used in nineteenth-century America', *Antiques* (Dec. 1972)
Gardner, Brian *The East India Company* Rupert Hart-Davis, London 1971 and McCall Books, New York 1971
Harvard, H. 'Papiers Peints', *Dictionnaire de l'ameublement* vol. 4
Hitch, H. J. 'Wallpapers', *Architectural Review* (Dec. 1948)
Hunter, George Leland *Decorative Textiles* Philadelphia 1918
Ionides, Basil 'Colour and Interior Decoration', *Country Life* (1926)
Jackson, J. B. *An Essay on the Invention of Engraving and Printing in Chiaroscuro* London 1754
Jenkinson, Hilary 'English Wallpapers of the Sixteenth and Seventeenth Centuries', lecture delivered before the Society of Antiquaries, 1925
Katzenbach, Lois and William *Practical Book of American Wallpapers* Philadelphia and New York 1951
Klingender, F. D. *Art and the Industrial Revolution* London 1947; reprinted Adams and Dart, Bath 1968, Paladin Books, London 1972 and Kelley, Clifton, N.J. 1968
Konody, Paul G. *The Art of Walter Crane* London 1902
'Lady Hertford and John James Audubon and the Chinese Drawing Room at Temple Newsam', *Leeds Arts Calendar* no. 61 (1968)
Leiss, J. *Bild Tapeten (aus alter und neuer Zeit)* Dortmund 1961
Lenygon, Francis *Decoration in England, 1660–1770* London 1914
Longfield, Ada K. 'Old Wallpapers in Ireland', *Journal of the Royal Society of Antiquities in Ireland* vol. 81 (1951)
   'Stucco and Papier Mâché in Ireland', *Journal of the Royal Society of Antiquities in Ireland* vol. 78 (1948)
   'Wallpaper and Legislation', *Journal of the Royal Society of Antiquities in Ireland* vol. 92 (1968)
MacCarthy, Fiona *All Things Bright and Beautiful: Design in Britain, 1830 to Today* Allen and Unwin, London 1972
MacClelland, Nancy *Historic Wallpapers* Philadelphia 1924
Musgrave, Clifford *Royal Pavilion: an Episode in the Romantic* L. Hill, London 1959
Nash, Paul *Room and Book* London 1932
Naylor, Gillian *The Arts and Crafts Movement* Studio Vista, London 1971 and MIT Press, Cambridge, Mass. 1971
Olligs, Heinrich *Tapeten, ihre Geschichte bis zur Gegenwart* Braunschweig 1970
Oman, C. C. *Catalogue of Wallpapers in the Victoria and Albert Museum* London 1925
Papillon, J. M. *Histoire et Practique de la Gravure sur Bois* Paris 1776

Pevsner, Nikolaus *An Enquiry into Industrial Art in England* 1937
Pioneers of Modern Design Penguin Books, Harmondsworth and Baltimore 1960
Quimby, Ian M. G. and Polly Anne Earl *Technological Innovation and the Decorative Arts* Winterthur 1973
Reade, Brian *Art Nouveau and Alphonse Mucha* London 1967
Rheims, Maurice *The Age of Art Nouveau* Thames and Hudson, London 1966
Sanborne, Kate *Old Time Wallpapers* New York 1905
Schmutzler, Robert *Art Nouveau* London 1962 and Abrams, New York 1964
Snook, Barbara *English Historical Embroidiery* Batsford, London 1960
Spencer, Isobel *Walter Crane* Studio Vista, London 1975 and Macmillan, New York 1975
Sugden, A. V. and J. L. Edmonson *History of English Wallpapers 1509-1914* London 1925
Trois Siècles de papier peint Musée des Arts Décoratifs, Paris 1967
Tunander, Ingemar *Tapeter* Stockholm 1955
Warner, Metford *The Notebooks of Metford Warner* (unpublished manuscript in the Victoria and Albert Museum library)
Waterer, J. W. *Spanish Leather* Faber and Faber, London 1971
White, Palmer *Poiret* Studio Vista, London 1973 and Clarkson N. Potter, New York 1973
Wyatt, M. Digby *Industrial Arts of the Nineteenth Century* London 1851

Index

Page numbers in italics refer to illustrations